AFTER THE BEAR PIT

Mark James
with Martin Hardy

This edition published in Great Britain in 2004 by
Virgin Books Ltd
Thames Wharf Studios
Rainville Road
London W6 9HA

First published in hardback in 2002 by Virgin Books Ltd

A catalogue record for the book is available from the
British Library.

ISBN 0 7535 0889 3

Typeset by TW Typesetting, Plymouth, Devon
Printed and bound in Great Britain by
Mackays of Chatham PLC

CONTENTS

FOREWORD

There are only three occasions on which Mark, my friend of 28 years, has asked me to do him a favour. The first was to be his best man when he and Jane were married in 1980; the second to be his assistant captain at Brookline; and now to write this foreword. Clearly his requests are decreasing with importance over the years and whilst happy to put finger to keyboard for this book, I truly wonder what he may ask me to do next.

Mark and I met on the practice putting 'brown' in Nigeria where we were to begin a friendship that instantly had all of the ingredients for a long and loyal bond. It has lasted to this day. The Nigerian Open in Lagos, February 1976, was the first overseas tournament for us both. My first tentative comment to Mark as he practised was 'What sort of club is that?' to which he replied in his usual dry style 'A putter!' With temperatures of over 100°F, a golf course that you cannot begin to imagine and an attempted military coup that left us housebound for three days, we had a lot to chat about. We quickly became soul-mates, room-mates and the terrible twosome about whom much has already been written.

The first favour can be quickly summed up by the scenario of Mark and I mistakenly in each other's top hat and tails. Add to that one of the shortest best man speeches in history, and the fact that I temporarily lost the bride's ring in the lining of my Moss Bros pocket, and you can begin to admire Jane's commitment to the man in her life, and her continued tolerance of our friendship.

The second came as even more of a surprise. The thought of a partnership in the Ryder Cup some twenty years since we had last donned the same team outfit, was both an exciting and nerve-racking prospect. Fortunately, it was only my toe that dipped into the 'Bear Pit' that week in September 1999 and, regardless of the outcome, it was to be one of my most memorable weeks in golf and a privilege to be have been involved at Brookline.

The third favour caused no sleepless nights. However, never having written a foreword before, and probably after this one never to write another, I decided to read a selection before I started. I came across words and phrases like 'unique', 'brilliant', 'unparalleled success', 'enviably talented' and 'the best'. Mark told me to put in what I wanted, so here goes.

Mark is a wonderful buddy with whom I have enjoyed endless practice rounds and travelled the world. He is one of golf's great putter testers, has a real edge to his sense of humour, is a steely competitor and has shown great bravery in his fight against cancer. It has been a lot of fun being a friend of Mark James. I have yet to read the book . . . so I look forward, as I hope you do, to what follows.

Ken Brown
February 2002

1. PISTE OFF

The words, when they finally came from a soft and unemotional voice, were delivered with care and consideration. They still hit me with all the force of a wrecking ball.

'It looks like lymphoma.'

Just four words, and my worst fears were realised. This would definitely mean one thing, and it was something for which I had not prepared myself. 'Damn!' I said, or words to that effect. 'No skiing for me this year.'

It may seem strange to some, but my first thoughts when hearing I had cancer were not that there was a possibility I might die or never play golf again, but that I would not be able to take in the heady air of the mountains and feel the crunch of powder beneath my feet during the winter of 2000/01. Along with *Star Trek* and gardening, skiing is a passion of mine, and I vowed then not to cancel one of my annual excursions on to the piste, merely to postpone it. It would be a pleasure I would return to after the fight against the Big C.

It might not exactly have been a relief to hear the doctor tell me what I had, but it did clear away the uncertainty that had been clouding my mind during months of discomfort and frustration. Being reasonably fit and healthy, or so I thought, I had struggled to come to terms with and understand why, for the first time in my life, I was suffering from unusual aches and pains in my back, none of which responded to different medicines, potions and treatments. I thought it might have been a bad case of indigestion. Little did I know a potential killer had settled in close to my kidneys.

I had no idea what I was returning to after a two-week holiday near Puerto Banus in southern Spain with my wife Jane, her sister Liz, Liz's husband Mark and their little girl Grace. I had done quite a bit of fitness work, mostly running, and played a bit of golf with Waddy, as Liz's Mark is called. I did have a few problems and intrusions into my holiday, but they had nothing to do with health; it was just the ongoing saga about the Ryder Cup and my involvement in the following year's match with the US as assistant to captain and close friend Sam Torrance. That saga I will deal with later. Suffice to say now that what happened prompted my resignation.

Now that the hassle was pretty much over, I came home in early August looking forward to the remainder of the season. I was feeling fine, not tired at all, even though it had been quite a tough summer with all the publicity surrounding my first book, *Into the Bear Pit*, and the controversy that attended it, but now I was rested up, rarin' to go and looking forward to playing golf. Ryder Cup points were starting in a couple of weeks' time, and having had a few good results early in the year I was eagerly anticipating a few chances to build on that encouragement so that I could challenge for a place in the side.

Having split with my long-time coach Gavin Christie earlier in the year, I had started work with Yorkshireman Pete Cowen, the swing sultan to several of the top Europeans these days after making his name with Lee Westwood and Darren Clarke particularly. I was looking forward to playing golf without distractions through the run-up to Ryder Cup selection. At 48, this may possibly have been optimistic, but you do need to have some purpose when you step on to the first tee and if I was not going to be there as an off-course assistant then it would be even better if I could make it as a member of Sam's on-course team.

Everything was settled and in place, but very soon afterwards I began to realise all was not as it should be with my body, although not once did I suspect that it might be life-threatening. It was more likely to be just a little bit of local discomfort, something a few painkillers or manipulation by the magic hands of the Tour's physiotherapists could put right.

The first symptoms developed at the Scottish PGA at Gleneagles between 24 and 27 August. I do tend to have a healthy appetite, although dieticians may argue against that, but I suddenly began to experience discomfort in the form of backache immediately after dinner. There was not too much to worry about because I had had a couple of vertebrae slip out of position earlier in the year and was subsequently prone to the odd twinge. The bones had needed a bit of manipulating back into place, so I just thought one of them had perhaps moved again slightly. I went to see Rob Hillman in the Tour's physiotherapy unit and told him to get cracking – encouragement that osteopaths and chiropractors the world over have little difficulty resisting.

I visited Rob a couple of times that week and he gave me every conceivable push and prod. He searched every bit of my back, even down into my upper thighs and sciatic nerves to try to see if there was anything wrong, but he pronounced my back in A1 shape. I thought nothing of it. Maybe it was just one of those things, a bit of occasional backache. After all, I'm not a teenager any more.

I played somewhere in the region of all right at Gleneagles and finished in the mid-20s – not too bad around that course, considering that it is a bit long, wide, wet and unsubtle for me. But by the time I arrived in Germany the following week for the BMW event, the backache not only persisted, but after every meal the discomfort was more acute. I went to see the tournament doctor and he took me into the locker room, laid me down flat and started feeling around in my stomach, generally trying to discover anything that might be the cause of my growing pain. After a thorough exploration, he came to the conclusion that I must have had some undigested food in my stomach and handed me a bottle. I had to put ten drops of this liquid in a glass of water and drink the mixture morning and evening, but it did not do the trick.

I don't do doctors very well, but I was at home briefly after the BMW and decided to go to see my general practitioner, Dr Stanley. It was the first time I had been to the local surgery in fourteen years.

I had been relatively lucky in my career, pretty much pain- and injury-free throughout. One of the few problems I had had was in 1999 – shingles, a condition that had developed immediately after I had agonised over my wild-card selections for the Ryder Cup team. Jane was convinced the complaint was a direct result of the mental anguish I had suffered in making those decisions and having to tell Bernhard Langer and Robert Karlsson that they had missed out. Generally, however, I have been very lucky because almost nothing has kept me out for any length of time at all. So I went to see Dr Stanley thinking that he would probably feel around my stomach, have a good listen and reassure me that it was just a bit of backache and nothing to worry about. It was getting slightly worse, but it still wasn't debilitating. The worst it got at that point was a sort of dull ache in my back after eating a fair-sized meal. It did not occur to me or anybody else that it might be something growing between my stomach and my spine.

Dr Stanley thought it might be stomach acid and put me on a drug called Losec, which is very widely used for such problems. I was to take the tablets for three weeks. I was only too pleased to follow his instructions because I was sure he had located the problem and that relief was soon to be had. But it wasn't long before I discovered we were still no nearer a solution, rather closer to discovering a terrifying truth.

That same week in early September I played in a kind of Celebrity-Am charity day at Fixby Golf Club in Huddersfield, and little did I realise the irony of the situation: the proceeds were to go towards cancer relief. Incredibly, I shot a 61 in about a 30mph wind on a course that is not particularly easy even in ideal conditions. I just could not stop the ball going in the hole no matter how hard I tried. It was certainly encouraging for my game.

Then, the same week, a worrying thing happened when I went running close to the Yorkshire moors where I live. I was with Jane and Liz, and although I am a reasonably efficient runner, I had to stop after we had gone only about four or five miles at a pace that was somewhere outside world record standard. Sometimes I do two or three miles quickly, but distance-wise I can do seven or eight without problems. After that the pace starts to reduce to little more than a crawl, but that day I had to stop for a minute because my back was hurting, and this time the reason was more difficult to understand because I had not just had a big meal. It was the first time it had started giving me problems in the normal course of my life. I was still taking the Losec, but without any noticeable change in my condition. Something was wrong, but what?

A few months earlier Jane might have found it more than amusing if I had had to stop during a run, but this time, following a couple of visits to the doctor, she started to worry – something she would do a lot more of come the winter. Jane and Liz were somewhat amazed because it's not like me to have to stop when exercising. I try to push myself very hard and can usually stagger along. I normally run between four and eight miles depending on who I'm with, and if I go to the gym I will do half an hour on the step machine, ten to fifteen minutes on the bike, run a few laps and do some weights and a bit of stretching. It's nothing hugely energetic, but doing it four or five times a week when I'm at home is enough to keep my body from falling apart. I don't do an awful lot of working out on Tour because after a five-hour round, a few hours' practice and bits and bobs, I tend not to feel too much like it, but if we are playing or staying in a nice place, I quite often go for a run. This time my run ended prematurely, and although I managed to jog back to base, it was not without discomfort.

By the time I got to Versailles on the outskirts of Paris for the Lancôme Trophy in mid-September, my general condition had not improved. Indeed, it was starting to deteriorate. My good friend and former Tour colleague Ken Brown, now a television pundit, had asked me to go and do a bit in the commentary box after my first round, but by now I was getting aches and pains more consistently during the day, although it was still worse after dinner. I decided to opt out of the television work and rest instead. Ken was working for the Golf Channel, which is broadcast in America, and quite often he commentates on his own, so it was disappointing to let him down.

Normally, if I'm playing in the morning, I will practise for an hour beforehand, play my round and then hit balls again for another couple of hours in the afternoon. You can get it done pretty quickly these days, unlike times not so long ago when we used to have to fight for space and turf and send our caddies out into the firing line. Thankfully, mainly thanks to Volvo's involvement in the Tour and the way they have improved our conditions since the mid-1980s to resemble those on the US PGA Tour, the days when caddies had to shag the balls are long gone. It used to be chaos in those days as the bagmen would stand out on the range trying to determine which were your balls and having to fetch them from here, there and everywhere, while getting hit by everybody else. It would take an eternity to hit a hundred balls, but today, with good turf, big practice areas and Titleist range balls, it is relatively easy to get on in the afternoon. It doesn't take too long to whack away a couple of hundred balls, then hit a few putts and chips.

But the pain was more consistent, although it was always worse after eating, so not only was I not practising as much, my eating habits were changing too. I was not having big meals any more. I was eating perfectly adequate amounts, but big meals would bring on the backache, so I avoided them. Not surprisingly, I played badly, missed the cut and headed out of France a little bit more concerned than I had been before.

Things did not improve when I arrived in Belgium for the Belgacom Open in the week beginning 18 September. I was now sitting down regularly on the course between shots, I was sleeping badly and I was eating considerably less, although probably still enough to get by without problems. I have always eaten quite large amounts on Tour, and always had a cooked breakfast when it was available: eggs, bacon, sausage, bread, orange juice, maybe some fruit first. This is followed by a reasonable lunch, normally egg and sausage sandwiches at the Caddie Shack. This outside hostelry is a particular favourite, and a lot of the players and most of the caddies go there for sustenance. It's usually situated behind the practice range, and Alan Stevenson and his crew serve up gourmet fast food and work on their latest golf inventions they hope will make them a fortune (fortunately for those on Tour they have not quite found anything yet that will enable them to quit their day job). For dinner, I can normally eat enough to feed an army, and although I do try to eat healthily it is an uphill battle. If we're on Tour then I'm doomed to failure, but if I do feel I'm getting too much fried stuff I will try to take in more vegetables, more salad and fewer whole animals.

At home, though, I eat very healthily. Most of the year I will have just toast for breakfast and soup and a sandwich for lunch, and for dinner a lot of vegetables are involved, albeit alongside a fair amount of meat. I figure what I do at home makes up for the excesses on Tour. Of course, a lot of food on Tour is comfort eating, so when I'm not playing too well the amounts tend to creep up.

In Belgium, at the magnificent links course of Royal Zoute, I was still taking the Losec, but my symptoms were getting worse. The only half decent thing that happened was being able to watch Lee Westwood hit balls on pro-am day. There were so many players practising, he just couldn't get on the range. I had just squeezed into a spot, so I took the opportunity of having a free lesson. I waved him in and watched him hit for half an hour so that I could try to learn something. What struck me was that he was hitting so few bad shots and the grouping was incredible. That's Lee's great strength when he's playing well: his bad shots are much, much better than most other professionals'.

I might have learnt something, but I could do little about it because my condition had got to the point where it was very uncomfortable. I played badly again – something with which I was becoming increasingly more familiar – and missed the cut. I was not hitting balls much at all, definitely not practising anywhere near as much as I should, but it was understandable in the circumstances. After I returned home from Belgium, on the Monday between the Belgacom and the German Masters I went back to my GP. I saw Dr Hyde this time – because Dr Stanley was unavailable – and told her that the Losec was not working. She booked me in for an ultrasound the following Monday. She'd wanted to send me that week but I was due to fly out to Germany the next day. I think she wanted to rule out problems with my gall bladder, but I cannot remember too much about the consultation because, to be honest, I really was not that worried.

Not once had I considered the possibility of cancer. Apart from my backache, I was still in reasonable shape and I was not tired. I just couldn't stand up for long without pain and I was sleeping badly, which is most unusual. Even during a Ryder Cup I can generally put my head down and get up to eight hours, no problem.

On the course at the German Masters I played with Michael Campbell for the first two rounds. He was fantastic, putting on an awesome display of shot-making that would allow him to go on to win the tournament easily. I was sitting down between every shot, couldn't practise for more than ten minutes without pain, and I wasn't eating an awful lot either. For the first time, I was starting to feel that I actually could not carry on with my job. I was not the least bit surprised to miss the cut fairly comprehensively.

On Monday 2 October I went in for the ultrasound at the Nuffield Hospital in Harrogate. It was the same kind of scan they do to look at unborn babies, although whatever my problems were I was fairly certain I wasn't pregnant. No sooner had the doctor put some jelly-like substance on my midriff and started looking than he said he could see something behind my stomach. After he had completed the scan, I asked him what he thought it could be. He said that he had noticed a large growth behind my stomach and that it was probably a lymphoma. I asked him optimistically if it could be anything else, and he said the only other alternative was a type of fever that attacks the whole body, but this was virtually unheard of outside the tropics.

It was probably while driving home from the hospital that I realised there was something seriously wrong with me. I knew I would not be going skiing as normal at the end of November. I was sure, too, that I'd have to stop playing for the rest of the season, so I would not be making any type of play for a Ryder Cup place. Basically, everything I was doing would have to come to a halt, and I would be involved with doctors for a long time.

The drive home is about half an hour, but it seemed like days. Jane is a reasonably good talker, but neither of us could find the right words. To be honest, we were relatively speechless. We still had no confirmation that it was a lymphoma, although the chances were that it was. Neither had we any idea what my survival chances were should it turn out to be cancer, or what sort of treatment I would need, whether it would entail operations or chemotherapy. We just did not know what time of day it was. We were stunned, and the silence between us reflected this.

The second of October 2000 – the day my life changed completely.

2. LOST BALL

I had no real idea what lymphoma was, although I was sure American golfer Paul Azinger had suffered from it in a shoulder and had made a full recovery. That was somewhat reassuring as I entered what was a difficult and uncertain period between getting the results of the ultrasound and starting chemotherapy on the penultimate day of October. There were 27 strange and particularly frustrating days in between. From the moment I discovered just how ill I was, all I wanted was to get on with the treatment. Nothing else mattered. I just wanted to get into hospital to start attacking the problem, whatever it was. The waiting seemed to make everything worse, not least my state of mind, although not once did I ever allow myself to think that I would not emerge from the other end of what seemed a long, dark tunnel. As ever, Jane was my guiding light throughout it all.

My weight was down to 12st 4lb, which is not exceptionally light, but I like to keep myself between 12st 8lb and 12st 10lb. I am very careful about trying to keep it in that band. If it goes one way or the other I will eat and exercise less or more, as necessary. I feel comfortable at that weight, and although I don't mind having a tiny bit of a belly, much above 12st 10lb I start to look a bit of a 'tubster'. Furthermore, sleeping was becoming much more difficult because I just could not get comfortable. Whenever I felt settled the pain would start again; if I nodded off for an hour, it was not a minute more.

That evening, following the ultrasound, Dr Hyde rang to let me know that she had booked me into the BUPA hospital at Roundhay in Leeds the next day, so that a bone marrow sample could be taken and a circuit-television-guided biopsy performed. A piece of the tumour needed to be removed in order to discover the exact type of cancer. I knew it had to be done, but it was a terrible inconvenience because I had to pull out of a couple of important engagements. One was for Nelson & Co., a local firm of solicitors. The senior partners are very close friends of ours and I was doing a company evening for them, and the following day was doing a golf day for my club sponsors Ping. I hate pulling out of commitments, especially at the last minute, so I was very annoyed at letting them down.

Having been to the Leeds General Infirmary in the morning for a CT scan, I checked into the BUPA hospital for the bone marrow extraction that afternoon, Tuesday 3 October. The procedure was performed under sedative, so I knew nothing about it until I woke up with a slightly bruised hip. Because my tumour looked like an advanced lymphoma, this could be diagnosed easily through testing my bone marrow.

The next day I was taken by ambulance back to the LGI for a CT-guided biopsy. A scanner is used so that the needle can be pushed through the back into exactly the right spot to pull out small pieces of tumour. The operation was performed by Alan Chalmers, who is a member of Alwoodley Golf Club, where I used to practise before moving over to Ilkley. I was sedated again, a process that does not completely knock you out but does put you on a different planet. It has about the same effect as ten pints of lager – you start talking rubbish. Alan said that I was complaining at having to go into Leeds with only six quid in my pocket. I am not sure what I was worried about, probably the fact that I could not afford a Big Mac and fries, twice.

I woke up in the ambulance, heading back to Roundhay, and couldn't even feel where the needle had gone in. Lymphoma specialist Dr Child came to my room that evening to tell Jane and me that he was fairly confident that I was indeed suffering from lymphoma and that any treatment would probably involve chemotherapy of some sort. Although not entirely certain what form any treatment may take, Dr Child was very encouraging and said that lymphoma was very responsive to chemo and that we should not despair. On that note, we returned home to wait from the phone to ring.

Having basically cancelled the rest of my year's work, Jane and I decided we had better issue a press release to explain why. We thought that making an announcement of our own would prevent too much rumour and speculation and also explain to the people I felt I had let down at Nelson & Co. and Ping just why I had pulled out of these events at the last minute. I didn't want people to get the impression that I just felt a bit tired and would rather put my feet up in front of the television than honour my commitments. Nothing could have been further from the truth.

The statement was short and simple: 'I have been diagnosed with lymphoma and pending further tests I expect to start chemotherapy soon.' I also asked the press to respect my privacy which, by and large, they did. I took a few calls but did not want to be bombarded. Before the release of the statement I spoke to the Executive Director of the European Tour, Ken Schofield, because as chairman of the committee I had to tell him that I would not be around for a few months and that Mats Lanner, my vice-chairman, would be presiding over any meetings until my return.

Those close to me already knew, of course. It is strange, but people just do not know what to say when you tell them, and it was definitely not easy breaking the news to my parents. I guess it must have been a bit of a nightmare for them, but they are generally optimistic people and I kept them informed of what was happening throughout. Their support and that of Jane's family was very reassuring.

We went back to Roundhay to see Dr Child a few days after the tests and he said that they had not obtained enough material from the CT-guided biopsy to pinpoint the exact type of tumour it was. However, by now he was no longer convinced that my problem was lymphoma. He thought there was a possibility that it may in fact be testicular in origin. Alan Chalmers could not believe that they did not have enough of the tumour. He had taken three million cells which had still proved insufficient material for a diagnosis. Dr Child referred me to surgeon Mr Paul Finan for a laparotomy, which is a full cut just under the breast bone right down to the lower navel, to allow a thorough search of the abdominal cavity. It would also enable them to pull out about an Oxo cube's worth of tumour for analysis.

Mr Finan is also a member of Alwoodley Golf Club and I was beginning to wonder if the golf club owned the hospital. What I knew for certain was that he has a great manner about him. He was very friendly, positive and calming. This would prove a great help through both this operation and indeed the one I was to have the following February. Paul examined me thoroughly. He must have been thinking that there could be testicular problems too as, like Dr Child had previously that afternoon, he examined mine. Paul also had a good look where the sun don't shine and, not finding anything of great interest, booked me in for an operation on 17 October.

It would be the first operation I had ever had in my life. Mr Finan outlined absolutely everything the two-hour procedure would entail. He told me basically that he was cutting me down the middle and would then work his way through to the tumour and chop a piece off – but not just any bit. Apparently, he would have to make sure that the sample was representative of the whole tumour, so he couldn't just go in and slice away willy-nilly. Thinking back to his examination of my testicles, I certainly didn't want him to chop away willy-nilly either.

I knew I was in good hands because I had been told that Mr Finan was the Tiger Woods of the surgery world. It was reassuring to know that he was not the Mark James of the surgery world, but to say I was apprehensive is the understatement of the year. On the 17th I would make my debut in the Leeds General Infirmary operating theatre, and I would discover if the first cut really was the deepest.

My thoughts were many and varied before the appointed day, but all I really wanted was for them to discover exactly what was wrong with me and to start treating it as soon as possible. I just craved a normal life again. I knew that in all probability, although I was just guessing, it would be some time before I would be able to resume normal service. I knew it would be months, but I did not know how many. I guessed everything would depend on the type of cancer and what treatment was necessary.

Paul Finan came to see me the evening before to put my mind at rest. 'Don't worry,' he said, 'I won't be having too much to drink tonight.' It was a sense of humour I appreciated, even though moments when I felt like laughing at that time were few and far between. Jane was with me as always, and we wiled away the rest of the evening watching television. There's just not much to chat about at a time like that – although the meaning of life might be appropriate – and besides, I was hardly sleeping at all and spending all the hours in the day in an exhausted stupor. I had started going to bed in the spare room and was spending virtually the whole night awake with the back pain. There were no other symptoms, just pure back pain. The growth was splaying both kidneys out sideways, pushing my stomach forward and my spine back.

The first thing I remember about going into hospital for the laparotomy was the pair of paper underpants they gave me to wear. I don't know who designed them, but whoever it was must have had eighteen pints and a bang on the head before he or she sat down at the drawing board. They certainly weren't meant to be worn by humans. Indeed, I'm not sure any type of being on this planet or any other would have found them a decent fit. You put them on, put a sort of gown over the top, and then hope that anybody who knows you doesn't see you. Then again, at a time like that what you look like is of little, if any, consequence.

I knew I was second up and just waited for them to collect me and wheel me through to the theatre. I was horrendously apprehensive. Actually, that is not really the correct term. I was plain shit-scared. The hospital staff could not have been better, though, and I remember chatting to them – one of them a golf fan, he told me – before going into theatre. Mr Finan popped round to say hello, all scrubbed up and ready. I had already had a needle stuck into me before going in, now it was just a question of administering the anaesthetic before starting the carvery. I don't remember what was going through my head before I went to sleep because I was shaking too much to have many coherent thoughts.

The operation started at about 2 p.m. and lasted longer than expected, about four hours. It must have been getting on for seven when I woke up in my room. Jane was there, but all I can really remember was feeling incredibly uncomfortable. I was in a lot of pain from the cut down the front, I was still suffering from backache and I was restless from the anaesthetic. I just could not settle mentally or physically at all. I would want to go to sleep, nod off, then wake up thinking I had slept for a couple hours and literally no more than 30 seconds had passed. I would do this on and off for the whole of the first night. I had to ring the buzzer and ask to be helped into a different position about every half an hour. The nurses must have been exhausted because every time I settled into a position I started to feel uncomfortable and would need to be moved. I would drift in and out of consciousness, drop off and wake up to see that the clock's minute hand had not yet gone through 60 seconds. It was terribly frustrating, but at least Paul Finan popped in to say that he had had a good rummage around, that all the organs looked in good shape, that the tumour was about ten by four inches and that it was probably a primary one. There was a good chance that nothing else was lurking out of sight. That was somewhat comforting, so now it was just a question of trying to recover.

Recovery was very, very slow. I think I was in hospital for about another week. It was a very tedious business, not helped because my stomach, which had been stitched back together with 30 staples, became infected and I started to shed some very strangely coloured substances. The scar was about fourteen inches long and just about as uncomfortable as I could stand. On top of that there was still discomfort from the tumour. Being unable to sleep for more than a minute was horrendous. To be honest, I was in bad shape.

My parents came to see me after the operation and my mother brought the biggest tray of fruit that has probably ever gone through hospital doors. I wanted desperately to set about it, but I was still on a drip and not coping too well at all. Mentally I was not great either. I knew there was no point in being overly depressed, but there didn't seem to be a huge amount of light in the tunnel, and if there was, I couldn't see where it was leading. I was trying to be as positive as I could, but I was desperate to know what was wrong with me, what treatment I needed to have. I just wanted it to start, to get it over and done with. At least I knew it was not an uncommon feeling because I received a letter from a chap who lives locally saying that he too had had cancer and one thing he remembered was being so desperate for the treatment to commence. They were my sentiments entirely.

The biopsy results didn't come through for about three or four days, although my memory of events at that time is still hazy. I was told that the tumour was testicular and that that was good news. I did not feel particularly elated, but they explained that it was something to be pleased about because cancer of the testicles is one of the most susceptible to chemotherapy.

At least now I knew exactly what and where the problem was and that I would be referred to Dr Bill Jones, an expert in testicular cancer, at the Cookridge Cancer Centre. I went to see him on 25 October and was taken straight from the hospital to the cancer centre a few miles away in an ambulance. Jane took her car to Cookridge, but the ambulance was better for me as it was door to door and I was not exactly sprightly. She met me there and we went to meet Dr Jones, who told me that I would be coming in to start chemotherapy on the 30th. The first session would last for five days, because initially they administer the drugs slowly to discover just how well or badly a patient's system reacts. A good response means subsequent sessions can be over a shorter period.

If there were two words that were truly frightening to me, one was cancer and the other chemotherapy, because I knew absolutely nothing about either. Now I had to face both of them.

Dr Jones examined me and felt my stomach gingerly because it was still hurting following the operation. He also felt my testicles and said that cancer in that region was becoming fairly common . . . a little more common than I was expecting or wanted. He said it was possible to have a testicular tumour of about two millimetres in diameter that shoots out seeds and then strangles itself through growing so quickly. I suppose this is why I had never noticed anything wrong with my testicles – not that I had been used to fondling them at regular intervals, not regularly enough anyway. Once the seeds are released they can travel around your body in either the blood or lymphatic systems. Mine travelled through the latter since there were no deposits elsewhere. If the seeds go via the blood, tumours in the lungs and brain are common and symptoms in these cases would be blood in the saliva or fits.

My chances of recovery, according to Dr Jones, were, I think, 90 per cent. Usually, I was told, for lymphoma the survival percentage is between 60 and 70, so it was reassuring to know my odds were already increasing. It was promising, but I was still apprehensive. He told me that normally the recovery rate for testicular cancer is 98 per cent, but because of the size of the tumour inside me, that had reduced it a bit. He was pretty confident that things would resolve themselves favourably. I know 90 per cent seems favourable, but that's still just nine out of ten surviving, and I'm not sure anybody would want to play at those odds. They were certainly better than fifty-fifty though, and I had no choice in the matter.

Dr Jones then explained exactly what cocktail I would receive for the chemotherapy. There would be three chemicals: bleomycin, etopaside and cisplatin, known as 'BEP', although not strictly an acronym as the cisplatin was actually platinum. He told me that bleomycin affects lung tissue and that it was possible I would lose some capacity during treatment. Tour de France winner Lance Armstrong had previously suffered from the same cancer as me, but his cocktail had not contained bleomycin after his first session. Obviously when you're cycling up the Alps you need every bit of lung capacity you can lay your hands on, but losing a bit of tissue is not crucial for chipping a ball back to the fairway. The drugs Lance took were harder for the body to tolerate, but for him it was worth it. He came back to win the Tour de France again, and his book *It's Not About the Bike* chronicles a fight by a man with an incredible will to win. In my case, the drugs Dr Jones had chosen were the ones most likely to cure me, and that was fine by me.

He also explained the side effects of the BEP regime: pins and needles in the hands and feet, hair loss, ulcers in mouth and stomach, weakened bone marrow, blotchy brown skin, red elbows and knees and lung fibrosis from the bleomycin. Bleomycin toxicity is the one thing that can kill a few patients, although in Britain if they detect a downward spiral they tend to back off on the treatment rather more quickly than on the Continent. Despite the seemingly endless side effects (at least there was nothing about putting in there; any change would have been an improvement anyway) modern chemo is nowhere near as bad as it used to be, but without putting too fine a point on it, I was still terrified at the thought of what I would have to endure, even though it was preferable to the alternative, and there was still about a week to go before the treatment was due to start.

My physical condition by this point had deteriorated to a stage where I considered myself skeletal. My weight was down to 11 stone; it had not been below about 12st 4lb since I was a teenager. To some extent I was starting to feel sorry for myself, but that was born out of the frustration at having to wait before starting treatment. I also looked horrendous, but Jane had plans in that direction. She started trying to fatten me up and gave me food with plenty of protein and carbohydrate. That way, she believed, I would be able to cope better with the chemo. The doctors were doing their bit so Jane thought we too should do everything we could to help.

These were extremely emotional times, and Jane was an enormous support for me throughout the treatment. Between the ultrasound and going in for the first chemo, I would have been tremendously lost without her. She has always been very, very strong mentally and she was essential to my recovery, and that is one of the reasons I always tried to put on a good face when we were together. I didn't cry much in front of her, but I would sometimes wake up in the middle of the night and crack up at the thought of perhaps not seeing her again. It is hard to remain strong all the time when you go through something like this, but having someone else staying strong and willing you to get better makes all the difference in the world. Jane was my difference, even though – and I didn't realise this at the time – she was only strong in my presence. Away from me, out would come the tissues.

Life had become much more of an emotional roller coaster than I had ever previously experienced. If I saw sad things, I would react more than normal, and the same would go for happy things. Someone might win a car on a game show or a gold medal at the Special Olympics, and I would be blabbing with joy for him or her. I suppose both Jane and I were in a fragile state.

What I did realise in hospital was that it wasn't always easy for two people who have always talked to one another quite a lot to communicate as readily. Never at any time during my illness did Jane and I broach the subject that I might not come through it. The possibility was too much for us even to think about. I certainly didn't want to consider it and I'm sure Jane felt the same. My attitude to the situation was simple. You hear people in similar circumstances making comments like 'I'm going to beat this thing', but I never felt like that or saw any reason for any overt displays of bravado. I just thought: 'I'm in the hands of these experts, I'll do my bit, and I'll try to eat enough to be fit enough to do what they want me to do.' I didn't suddenly develop a belief in the Almighty. I had complete faith in the doctors for they were the people who were in control. The LGI is a renowned hospital and the Cookridge Cancer Centre is one of the best facilities of its type. It certainly helped to be told this before going into these places. I know you hear a lot of bad things about the NHS, but I was treated partly private, partly on the NHS, I had all my chemo on the NHS, and from what I saw they were absolutely fantastic. The treatment at Cookridge was so good, it was nothing short of remarkable.

Jane and I kept on the positive side, and once we had seen Dr Jones and he had said survival chances were 90 per cent we felt a lot better about the situation. We could see the light, however faint. Between four and six chemo sessions would take us through to about the end of January 2001. Now it was just a question of Jane trying to build me up and me trying to cope with the waiting. My future was in the hands of the doctors, so all we could do was concentrate on getting me as strong as possible to deal with the chemo.

My stomach had shrunk, but I still had a tumour that was growing and forcing my kidneys out so there was still plenty of pain and discomfort. On top of this, in spite of having had the staples taken out my stomach was still infected and I was on antibiotics. Jane continued trying to feed me up, but it was difficult because I was suffering. It was not a good time for me. All I wanted to do was sit in front of the television. I would try to walk down the road, up to half a mile a day, but it was a slow process and for the first time in my life I felt very old. I also looked it – at least that's what I saw when I looked in the mirror. I remember saying to myself, 'You look 60, and not a great 60 at that.'

Although I had heard about chemotherapy and been told about it, when the appointed day finally arrived and I signed into Cookridge, I honestly didn't know what to expect. I had been told about people being sick for days and I couldn't stop thinking about all the different chemicals they were going to pump into my body. I knew it was something I had to do, and wanted to do, but I was not looking forward to it at all.

That Monday morning, 30 October, came and Jane drove us the fifteen minutes to Cookridge. The first snow of the winter was falling and the signpost to the cancer centre was completely white. As usual, the snow soon turned to rain, and two days later it took Jane one and a half hours to get home because of flooding. I checked in at reception and they sent me up to Fleming Ward where I dropped off my case, music and books and various other bits and pieces that would help occupy the long hours.

It should have come as no surprise that the first thing I had to do after being admitted was have a blood test. This was about the eighty-fifth time in the last month and I was starting to run out of veins. They were testing for things like red blood cells and iron levels – things that can sometimes be too low for the body to withstand chemo. They were also looking for certain protein markers that are only present when there is a tumour – except for someone on steroids or cannabis. One athlete in the past did test positive for steroids when in fact he had testicular cancer. My protein markers were low, which meant the tumour was slow-growing and could have been around for several years. The blood results came in an hour or two later and I was pronounced ready for action.

First they weighed me, a process that allows them to tell easily if the body starts to retain a lot of liquid. Platinum, in particular, affects the kidneys. When it was first used it often killed patients through renal failure, then some clever fellow suggested flushing the chemicals through on a tidal wave of water so that the platinum did not have a chance to damage the kidneys. Water also flushes out potassium and magnesium, so the large amounts of saline that are put through the body before, during and after the tumour-killing chemicals contain these two essentials. If the body starts to retain the water the chemicals could cause damage. This happened to me during one session and I had to pee ten times in the following hour and a half after they shot some rocket fuel into me to get things moving again.

After getting weighed I was put on a saline drip, first with magnesium and then potassium. After a few hours of this it was time for the real thing. First came the anti-sickness drugs. One of them had to be administered slowly because it can apparently make your backside tingle (I was never tempted to ask them to put it in quickly to discover what I was missing). As soon as they were in my system, the chemicals followed.

I was actually waiting for the experience of having to rush off and throw up, but that feeling never came at all. Throughout all the chemo sessions I was only sick twice, and both times were first thing in the morning. I never lost my appetite, and although unfortunately there was no fish and chip shop outside, thankfully the food was an awful lot better in Cookridge than at Leeds General, where it was suspect to say the least and did not taste very nice. They have had gastronome Loyd Grossman in since to revamp hospital food. They certainly needed to at LGI, but Cookridge was not bad at all. There was plenty of chocolate at my disposal, and bacon for breakfast on Thursdays was a major result, but there are few bonuses when you are fighting cancer.

I felt fine after the first day, although still tired from the operation and the chemicals. I got more and more tired throughout the period of chemo, and consequently it took me longer and longer to recover. Sometimes the infusing machine would start beeping – probably because it didn't like the etopaside because it had bubbles in it. I would try to shake them out of the line or give the machine a tap without risking plunging the hospital into darkness, but somehow I never got it to stop making a noise for any length of time. The infusion pump, to give it its proper name, basically monitors the pressure in the vein and, apart from delivering the chemicals at the right speed, acts as an early-warning system for obstructions, bent pipes or something like an abscess. In days gone by a simple drip was used and by the end of the week the treatment could be as much as twelve hours behind.

The staff at Cookridge were absolutely fabulous and really seemed to enjoy their job whatever it entailed. They were always cheerful, and it does make a difference when they are like that, especially when you're not feeling 100 per cent. They really were tremendous and made you feel it was a vocation for them rather than a job.

I soon got into the routine not only of hospital life, but also daytime television. Unfortunately, after 9 a.m. the only thing to do with the television was switch it off. I could not take Kilroy seriously and I found Richard and Judy a bit annoying, but it would always come back on at one o'clock for the news. Things picked up a bit later in the afternoon with *Through the Keyhole* and *Fifteen to One* followed by *Countdown*, or I could watch *Ready, Steady, Cook* and then *The Weakest Link*. It is amazing how you can get locked into these things. I would get really annoyed if anybody interrupted because for me this was the best part of the day.

Being in hospital with little to do apart from feel the chemicals go through my body did give me time to think, and one thought preoccupied me particularly: 'God, I haven't done the dahlias!' It was a bit late because come the second week of November, living in Yorkshire, we had already been having frost for at least a month. I hadn't felt up to doing it to be honest after the first lot of chemo, but it would have been cruel to carry on like that. I love dahlias. I always think of them as a man's kind of plant – completely unsubtle and obvious, but a nice splash of colour. So as soon as I could I went out to bring the dahlias in. It was still hurting to bend over, but I managed to dig them all up, jet spray and dry them out in the greenhouse before packing them in boxes of peat. It was all I could do to carry the boxes into the garage.

However much I was into the routine of hospital life, it was always great to come back home. After the first dose of chemo I was tired for three days, and I developed a squeaky voice. They had warned me about hair loss, which was something I was more able than most to cope with, but they hadn't warned me that I might sound as if I'd been inhaling helium for a week. In fact, there was no noticeable hair loss at the time, although it was, I must say, difficult to determine if I had lost any more of my few remaining strands. The only effects seemed to be the tiredness and the squeaky voice. There was an immediate bonus, however: the most noticeable change was that for the first time in a long time I was in almost no discomfort from my back. What a relief to know that the treatment was having an immediate effect on my tumour and that I could finally sleep! Progress was being made, slowly but surely. The light was getting gradually brighter, although still not at more than a 60-watt glow.

I was never short of well-wishers throughout the fight. Almost as soon as we made the announcement about my illness I started to receive letters, while friends would ring to check on me. I spoke regularly to Sam Torrance and other European Tour colleagues and friends such as Mark Roe, Jamie Spence and Gordon Brand Jnr. I remember one of those visits when I was at Leeds General particularly clearly. The other Brand – Gordon J. – and his wife Lyn came to visit me one Sunday afternoon just when the Grand Prix highlights were on. It was the first good thing I had seen for ages, but with just four laps to go until the end of a thrilling race Gordon told me who had won. He was not even trying to be funny, he was just being Gordon.

Many of our close friends popped into the LGI to say hello. Andrew Mair, my golf design partner, made the trip home to Newcastle from Preston via Leeds – not the easiest route in the world. He brought me some thermals because he had had a similar operation many years earlier and remembered feeling cold for weeks. His memory was accurate. I did shiver for a long time after the first operation, unless I was well wrapped up or next to a large fire. Mark Roe brought me a singing fish. It was noisy, but not as noisy as Roey. The effort all these people made to come and see me did me a lot of good. Jamie Spence even drove up from Kent for the day just to see how I was.

I was also getting loads of cards, including one from Nick Faldo (I hoped our feud was well and truly over) and some of the Ryder Cup Committee, several of whose members I had described in not particularly complimentary terms in the newspapers. It was therapeutic to speak to some people, to explain what was happening and what I was going through. It is not an easy thing to do, but it did prove a big help and somehow made things easier. Some had trouble knowing what to say, but I'm not great on the phone anyway, so occasionally it was a little difficult. But people had taken the trouble to lift up the telephone even though they had realised it would not be easy, so that was very kind.

In the main, it was pretty much just my close friends who rang me – that's all I would have wanted, to be honest – but I was pleased to take a few calls from Gary Hart, who works for Ping in the USA. Gary had had cancer over a number of years and come through it and he rang me several times from America. It was great to speak to someone who had been through much, much worse than me. You know immediately that they know what they're talking about and understand what you're going through. It was also nice to hear from another old friend, David Feherty. My former Tour colleague, now a cult figure on American television, sent me an email that read: 'If you die, I will be really, really cross.' It was much appreciated, a rare moment of light relief at a time when there were precious few of them.

I was also sent a couple of books. Dave Musgrove, veteran top-flight caddie and book collector, sent me C.S. Forester's *Hornblower and the Atropos* – a 1954 edition. It was a departure from my usual science fiction and golf diet but was a really excellent read. Ken Brown sent me *My Greatest Day in Golf* by Darsie L. Darsie which contained a story about Eddie Loos, a young New York City pro who, down on his luck, once slept in a sand trap and was never afraid of them again. We had always found this amusing – it was one of the few tactics we never employed.

Within a few weeks I was feeling a little better and stronger. I went to see Dr Jones, who put me back down on the bed and felt around my stomach. He said that the tumour had already shrunk noticeably, which was very encouraging. I guessed it had to some degree because of the back pain easing, but to hear him confirm it was to say the least heartening. I also had a blood test while I was in for the consultation; amazingly, the results came through in about ten minutes, sent from the blood lab up to his office by computer. The doctor said that my iron was a bit low and told me to get some steaks and red meat inside me ready for the next chemo. Apparently, if the iron levels in your blood are not high enough then they will not let you go in for chemo. I would have been gutted had that happened because I wanted the chemo as often as possible. It was obviously having some effect.

Constant checks were also kept on my weight, and every time I went to the toilet I had to pee into a jug, measure it and then log it in a file hanging from the bottom of the bed. I also had to measure everything I drank and write that down so that it could be checked to ensure I had the right amount of body fluids. The register also contained details of the drugs I was taking and all the potential side effects. I made the mistake of reading it once. The file contained about 150 items of information I was unaware of. I did not read it again.

Even though I felt progress was being made, there was still a niggling thought at the back of my mind that I was having all this stuff pumped into me and that it was not going to do any good at all. That had been the case with the Losec, so it could happen again. I understood that this time it was different and they knew what the problem was and how to deal with it, but occasionally I would think, 'What if this does not want to be cured?' Thankfully, Dr Jones was pleased with my progress, assured me I was doing fine and told me to return for my next cocktail of chemicals on 20 November. We parted in a much more upbeat and optimistic manner because we knew we were going in the right direction and the symptoms were in retreat.

My recovery from the laparotomy was also progressing well, albeit slowly, and Jane and I were trying to do as much walking, or rather I was trying to do as much walking, as we could. Although I still wasn't a contender for the British marathon squad, it was some exercise. As we shuffled along the roads close to our home we had but one hope, that this thing would just melt away and I would be cured. It is a strange feeling being positive about recovery yet being aware that there is a chance things will not turn out well. Knowing that my chances were good and that the chemo was working made the mental side of things easier. Although occasionally we had the feeling the goalposts were moving, I never had any real setbacks during treatment and that also helped considerably.

Eating was not so much of a trial now because I was getting no after-effects as a result of having a big meal. Jane continued to feed me with red meat and vegetables and I was getting a fair bit down me. I was doing very little else, and I was starting to realise that it might be quite a long time before I played golf again. Even after six sessions of chemo it would still take a while to recover and I might not be back on Tour until April 2001. I also began to think about the money side of things, but fortunately my last book did very well so I was getting royalties from that, and Ping honoured my contract even though I didn't play as much as I was contractually obliged to, for which I was very grateful. It means an awful lot to a professional golfer when something like that happens. All of us on Tour live in fear to some extent that one day we may have to face the prospect that we just might not be able to play as well or get ill and not be out there for months. For Ping to keep paying me in full was fantastic. Glenmuir, also, treated me more than fairly, and it was a big weight off my mind knowing that some money was coming in.

Jane's diet slowly began to work and I put on a wee bit of poundage, although the eleven and a half stone I had reached by mid-November was still more than a stone below my fighting weight. Blood tests prior to my second session of chemo revealed I had adequate amounts of everything, and that was a relief. Had they been inadequate, I could have been prevented from continuing the treatment or, to get me through, they might have given me a series of intra-muscular injections in a leg. I didn't ask too much about them because I just didn't fancy whatever they entailed, end of story. Chemo kills healthy as well as malignant cells, but normal cells have the ability to regenerate. Bone, for instance, is totally replaced every two years, red blood cells every four months. Most tissues of the body except muscle, brain and kidneys regenerate. The normal recovery process hopefully gets everything strong enough to withstand the next session, otherwise injection or a delay is the order of the day. Fortunately, I avoided both, so it was back into Cookridge for what would be the same amount of chemicals, but this time over three days rather than five. They figured my system was ready for a faster fix.

I guess you're more likely to suffer ill effects if the chemicals are put in non-stop, but the powers-that-be decided that I was fine and, sure enough, there were no ill effects. The only problem for me was the infusion pump which was placed on a rickety old stand and had to be dragged everywhere.

Every time I finished a chemo session I felt tired and suffered from squeaky voice syndrome, but the symptoms of the tumour were completely gone. I didn't get backache at all, and we were very optimistic. I saw Dr Jones at the end of November and he had a deep feel around my stomach again and thought the tumour was already down to one third of its original size. That really did cheer us up, considering that when we started out it had measured ten inches by four inches. Two thirds had gone, and that was a great feeling.

Blood tests after this latest session showed that I was a wee bit low on salt, so we felt forced to go out and buy a lot of crisps. Even so, I was given a blood transfusion because generally my levels were pretty low. The new blood gave my immune system and red blood cell count a boost and put a bit of colour into my now grey skin.

I was hoping four sessions would be enough to make the thing disappear. It seemed to be doing pretty well, and I knew that there was a small chance that if it didn't disappear I would have to have another operation to remove the remnants of the dead tumour. Apparently, even though a tumour can be completely dead, it is possible for it to regrow after a period of time. One of the things that had intrigued me was why they didn't just cut the tumour out. It was a question I put to Paul Finan, and he told me that basically a tumour is like superglue: as soon as it touches something it sticks to it and grows on and around it. It has a rubbery consistency and a skin which feels very much like orange peel. It is impossible just to cut it off.

The third session started on 11 December and was very similar to the second, but afterwards Dr Jones told me another two would probably do it, though I might indeed need the operation to remove the remnants of the dead tumour. It did worry me that this would be similar to the earlier laparotomy I had undergone which had taken a long time to recover from.

It was not the greatest Christmas I have ever spent. I didn't have massive energy reserves or the desire to go out on the lash as per normal, but we were buoyed by the reaction of my body and the doctors to the treatment so far. We stayed at home most of the time, but we went to have Christmas lunch with the Waddies. My spirits were fine. We knew we were getting on top of it and it was great to see a lot of friends at Liz's for pre-dinner drinks. I hadn't really been circulating much for a couple of months, so now what they'd heard on the grapevine they could get first hand.

Nobody commented on my appearance, although by now much of my hair had fallen out just about all over my body. My eyebrows had gone, as had virtually every other area of hair on me apart from the occasional strand here and there. My moustache was still hanging on because that is where my hair growth is strongest, but it too went during the fourth chemo session. It was around this time that my good friend Mark Roe – occasionally he acts in a manner that could be construed as certifiable – decided to send me a wig, false eyebrows and moustache. They always say it's the thought that counts. He even put in a note asking for a photo of me wearing them. I did not oblige. A sense of humour like Roey's needs no encouragement.

The fourth and what turned out to be the final chemo session started in the new year on 2 January and went pretty much as before. I was an old hand by now. I would go in on the morning for the blood test and return home for lunch, ring up at 2 p.m. to check that the results were OK and go straight up and get weighed and plugged in. I could also work the infusion pump now, squeezing the last drops out of the bag just like the nurses did. I was never too keen on handling the cisplatin, however. This came in the same kind of plastic bag as the other chemicals but was covered in a red collar. It made it look radioactive, yet this was the stuff that really revolutionised the treatment of testicular cancer in the late 1970s and early 1980s. Before 1982 I would probably have died from my illness, so I was grateful for the big difference platinum made.

On the back of work by Melvyn Samuels in Texas, it was Lawrence Einhorn who pioneered treatment by platinum, vinblastine and bleomycin. Patients were frequently incapable of doing up their shirt buttons because of the neurotoxicity of vinblastine, so that was eventually replaced by etopaside, leading to the BEP regime. These days, with the lower toxicity of the treatment, the flushing-out technique and ever-improving anti-sickness drugs, fewer than 10 per cent of patients suffer much in the way of nausea and the cure rate is 98 per cent. I was glad I was born in 1953 rather than 1933.

I had a CT scan after the last session, then went back to see Dr Jones. He told me that although the tumour had been shrinking all the time from the chemo, on this occasion it had not altered at all. My heart sank, but was immediately raised when he added, 'That's probably because it's dead.' You cannot imagine how good that sounded – that the thing had actually been killed. I don't think he deliberately knocked me over and then built me up again, but I have rarely, if ever, experienced two such contrasting emotions within the space of a few seconds.

Dr Jones saw no reason to send me back for another cocktails session so the only thing left to me was a return into the good hands of Paul Finan for the operation to remove the remnants of the tumour. Although it was dead, or necrotic (difficult words are the norm in hospitals), the remaining matter, or necrosis, just might regrow if I was unlucky. Paul said he would bring in Adrian Joyce, who was also a Tiger Woods in the world of surgery, apparently. If Paul said he was brilliant, that was good enough for me. They would be assisted by a Mr Gough, a vascular surgeon, because a dead tumour is much more solid and they were going to have to cut it off because it was wrapped around the arteries to the kidneys. There was a slight complication in my case in that whereas generally there are one or two arteries to each kidney from the main blood supply that goes down your spine, I had three, and all were tied up in the dead tumour.

I felt a lot more optimistic than I had before my first operation. The treatment had gone well and physically I would be a lot more able to withstand an operation. Although I had not been able to go to the gym during my chemo sessions because of the biomycin affecting the lung tissue, Dr Jones said I could start working out about two weeks after I had finished with the chemo and that gave me a fortnight to get some fitness back for the respiratory check before going in for the operation. I felt all right. I had had no colds or flu the whole winter and that was a really good break. My resistance was obviously very low, but I didn't get ill at all.

The second and hopefully final operation was scheduled for 8 February, which meant that another skiing excursion might have to be postponed. Not only do we go early season, but often also late season; this time we had arranged to go with some friends, Andrew and Alison Linden, and their boys Tom, Harvey and William, together with Steve and Chris Thompson. The plan was to go early April, and the fact that Paul Finan had kindly managed to allocate some of his precious time to me earlier than might have been expected gave us hope that we might be able to go after all. We normally rent one big apartment, and the boys are dead keen and all top-class skiers, so I was really hoping to be fit for it. When you've been stuck in a house or hospital all winter it is, I imagine, like being in prison. You can't wait to get out. The Lindens and Thompsons wanted to go out around 5 or 6 April; Jane and I were thinking of maybe going out earlier, then meeting up with the others when school holidays and financial years allowed.

There was not long or far to go now with the treatment, but still the messages of support came flooding in. I received hundreds of letters and get-well cards. They came consistently right through the winter, and it was of great help to read them. Just to know that people are thinking of you means so much. I know there are people who are worse off and who put up with tougher things, and even fail to come through, but it is great to know that people have taken the trouble to send a card or a letter.

I worked out for two weeks, then went in on the 6th for a respiratory test that consisted mainly of blowing into tubes. Being able to work out again was unbelievable, despite being very tough. Running felt like I had lead in my shoes. I just couldn't get going at any speed at all. The level I was doing on the step machine was embarrassingly low. I couldn't do it for more than about six minutes, and that was incredible. I was completely out of shape. The after-effects from the initial operation were still taking their toll, and those from the last chemo had also continued longer than normal. It had taken me a good week to get over the squeaky voice, and I would feel dizzy for five or six seconds if I got up too quickly. Nevertheless, at the end of the test I was given a rating of 86. I don't know if that was out of 100, but I was told it was reasonably normal so I must have made some progress in the gym and recovered a wee bit of fitness.

The day before the operation they had to clean my bowels out. I was given a very interesting fluid called

Klene-Prep; I had to drink about six pints of the stuff. It tasted like sulphuric acid and iron filings. Afterwards, for about an hour and a half you think nothing's happening, then you spend the next three hours on the loo. It definitely got rid of everything from my system, and this was vital for the operation because they don't want any food hanging around. I was amazed to discover later that after they cut you down the middle, they lift all the intestines out – and there must be about ten miles of them – and put them on a table by the side to keep them out of the way.

Before the operation Mr Joyce came by to check on me. Presumably as a 'better safe than sorry' tactic he put a star and an O near my left testicle and an asterisk and an H on my right side where a hernia was going to be repaired at the same time. The main operation was termed a retroperitoneal node dissection – the cutting away of the dead bits of the tumour from around my arteries to the kidneys. I was also in for an orchidectomy, which translates into the removal of the left testicle. In between chemos they had done an ultrasound on my testicles to locate the scar because they knew there had to have been a tumour on one of them at some stage. The doctor hadn't been able to find anything at all, so they'd sent the pictures away to be looked at by an expert. It was only a small scar, so obviously it was a minute tumour that had caused all the problems. I had no great feelings about losing my left testicle. I felt that after all the trouble it had caused me it was the least it deserved. I would have barbecued it for several days given the chance. I wasn't sad to say goodbye.

It was suggested that I have a couple of epidurals as pain relief during the operation because I had reacted so badly to the morphine the last time. I didn't particularly fancy having wires thrust into my spine, but anything would be better than the agonies of the first operation. For some reason, as I was wheeled from my room through ten miles of corridors at the LGI, I got more and more nervous. I thought that when I got to the theatre they might refuse me on the grounds that I was sweating too much, but they got the wires in through my quivering back and then knocked me out with the old anaesthetic.

Five or so hours later I woke up to discover that I looked like a diagram of the London Underground system. I had never seen so many lines in all my life. I also still had all the wires in my back from the double epidural, plus two in my left arm and one in my right that had a red and white line shooting up into a machine. I had a drain in my stomach and one in my groin and a massive sort of adapter thing in my neck with three lines coming out of it and heading off into another machine. I felt like something out of a sci-fi movie. With all these things coming out of me, the most amazing thing was that I was in absolutely no pain at all, not the least bit uncomfortable or restless like I had been after the first operation. Jane was there. Paul Finan had already spoken to her and said that everything went well. She knew the score while I just kept drifting in and out of sleep. I felt tremendously comfortable, more so than Jane, who left late in the evening to find her car had been broken into while she had been visiting. The only thing missing was the CD player which must have been worth all of £20 second hand. Makes you wonder why they do it.

Everything seemed to have gone reasonably well, though they hadn't quite been able to remove all of the tumour.

Fortunately, the subsequent biopsy showed that it was completely dead. Although there was a small chance of something growing from that dead tissue, they considered the risk wasn't worth any more operations. To completely get rid of what was left they would have had to remove a kidney and the associated arteries, so they decided to bide their time, chart my progress and send me for regular scans.

I had put on a massive amount of weight – my end of the settee was never without a tub of Miniature Heroes throughout the winter – but not much of it was muscle because I had just been sitting on my backside for a couple of months. Jane's build-up plan had worked so well that I was back to my normal 12st 7lb by Christmas, but subsequently I had put on another stone. Trying to reverse it when you have been putting on weight like that is incredibly difficult. I wasn't shedding much in the gym because I couldn't do a huge amount of working out. I was a real 'tubster' when I went in for that second operation.

I was kept on a double epidural for a day or so and my recovery was fantastic. I was in Leeds Infirmary's intensive care unit and was never comfier than when sleeping. I had been warned that when they take your bowels out for the operation and stuff them back in they tend to seize up and nothing happens for about five days. About 36 hours after the operation mine wanted to start working again, so they had to whip me off the epidural and lift me on to a portable loo – not the most dignified of manoeuvres and something I could have done without in one respect, but not in another. The last remnants of the Klene-Prep were obviously still in my system.

After two days in the ICU I was moved back up to my room, and I had a great view out. They had erected an ice rink in the centre of Leeds and I enjoyed watching the skaters. My turn was not that far away, I hoped. I was feeling well and I was up and walking very, very quickly. I felt so fit that I was shouting to go home after about five days. I couldn't see the point in staying in hospital. I was not in that much pain, I was eating, everything seemed to be working normally and I was walking up and down the ward without serious pain or discomfort. They finally relented, and I was home in less than a week. It had taken longer to get out of hospital after the first op, but this time I felt great and the wound hadn't got infected. I needed fewer painkillers and was off them completely very soon after coming home. Then again, I did have an incentive. The ski slopes were calling, and I had every intention of answering them.

When I got home, I went straight on to a diet because the only thing I had that would fit me were joggers and I figured they would look pretty daft when I rejoined the Tour. I had visions of spending the rest of my life in a shell suit or a pink velour cat suit because I was the shape of a Teletubbie. After my first operation I had gone from 12st 4lb to 11 stone in ten days. I was hoping for something similar this time round. I went into hospital at 13st 7lb, and when I weighed myself at home I was 13st 5lb – I had lost just two pounds. Taking into account the loss of a dead tumour and a bollock, I had got fatter. On the plus side, the only physical problem I had was that I kept pulling stomach muscles. It wasn't the wound trying to give way, just that I kept pulling odd muscles when I sneezed or blew my nose.

But I was progressing, and the thin mountain air was beginning to invade my nostrils again. Within a few weeks

I felt fit enough to ski, and on 23 March Jane and I flew to Colorado where we stayed for three weeks. The Lindens and the Thompsons joined us for the last ten days, and Tom, Harvey and William certainly put me through my paces. I was anticipating taking it easy at the start of my holiday, but that lasted about one morning. As soon as the others arrived, the boys started dragging me down some fearsome runs, showing off their natural technique – a skill or knack you get when you start skiing at a younger age than 39, which is when I started. I don't think I've ever enjoyed a holiday more in my life. I was in some discomfort and had bandages round my stomach through-out the trip, but it was well worth it. Jane and I were starting to get our lives back.

I had been working out at the gym from the beginning of March – gently at first, but increasing the tempo quite quickly. I was pulling stomach muscles for several months, but only slightly, nothing to worry about. The time was approaching when I would be able to set a date for my comeback to the golf course, although I wondered about the potential psychological drawbacks to playing fairly quickly after such a traumatic period of my life. I tried not to rush back and didn't hit balls until a week or so after we returned from Colorado. By that time it was nearing the end of April, and I decided the Volvo PGA Championship at Wentworth at the end of May would be a suitable event and venue to see if I could still hack it.

In retrospect, returning there did make things really difficult for me because the West Course at Wentworth is a tough cookie and in 2001 played host to a very strong field, but the two tournaments after that were at Woburn and Forest of Arden, also very good tests, so there could be no easing my way back in. On the other hand, it did get me into the swing again at the right time.

My walk back into the spotlight came earlier, however, because I received a letter from the BBC wondering if I would like to do some commentary at the Benson & Hedges International at the Belfry starting 10 May. I think they had been looking for a new face, and my good friend Ken Brown had put my name forward. I had been behind the microphone before when I worked a couple of times for Eurosport, and it was work I quite enjoyed. The highs are not as high as when playing golf, but the lows aren't as low either, so that's not a bad bargain. I agreed to make my debut for the Beeb.

I had been back for a base scan that April, the first since the operation, and I returned for another three months later. Afterwards Dr Jones sat down with me. There is a great feeling of relief when the results give the all clear because in the few days coming up to a scan I am at best edgy. Waiting for Dr Jones following his meeting with his colleagues was, to say the least, tense. I need not have worried. The second scan showed that what was left of the tumour was gradually dissolving and they decided that they should take no further action. There was every chance that the remaining tissue would cause no problems, and they decided just to monitor me every three months to see how things were progressing. The alternative was a kidney transplant or removal, but Dr Jones believed that the cancer was unlikely to reappear, and that if I was kept under supervision any sign of life in it could be dealt with quickly enough anyway. It seemed to me to be the sensible course of action. What was the point of going in unless they absolutely had to and they had already got public footpath signs in my stomach saying 'Surgeons this way'?

I could now get on with my life. My attitude is not that much different now because I think I was fairly laid back and I really did enjoy life beforehand – not in the sense of going out, getting drunk and partying all the time, just in the sense that I do enjoy what I do, I love being married to Jane and I take pleasure in life the way it is. Although it's bad luck being ill, to be honest I felt lucky and still do. Much worse things happen to millions of people and I have probably come through it unscathed. I'd had help of course – the NHS, the doctors, surgeons and nurses, friends and family. They were all fantastic. And then there was Jane. Every day in hospital after my operations she was there. Every day during chemo she was there. And every day during the long winter she catered to my grumpy whims and kept my brain unscrambled. I am lucky to have come through the illness, but I had a lot of help from a lot of people, particularly Jane.

3. BACK ON COURSE

I had wondered if my ordeal had given me a new perspective, particularly professionally, and that is why I did not try to rush back into playing too quickly. I thought that psychologically I might need time to adjust to getting over the illness and starting back, but I honestly don't think too much has changed, although if I three-putt nowadays I can just say that things are not relatively speaking that bad. My attitude on the course has definitely not been affected. I am still trying as hard and I am still as keen to do well. My ambitions may have changed somewhat with age, but there is still ambition there and I have a fairly burning desire to compete and do better than I have been doing.

These days golf, like most sports, has turned into a young man's game because of the distance the ball is being hit. These kids have been taught all their lives to pump iron and hit the ball with every muscle of their body going into it. They have learnt to smash the ball out there and carry it 280 to 290 yards. The older players among us didn't learn to play the game that way, and it is very, very difficult to adapt. There is hardly anyone on Tour over the age of 40, apart from dy Lyle, who is capable of playing that way. Most of us learnt to play with persimmon heads, certainly with wooden heads – persimmon if you were lucky – and you couldn't jump at the ball because if you missed the middle the ball would go sideways. Now the heads of these clubs are so big there is an enormous sweet spot. If you're a bit out one day, you can still get the ball away, so although I have a desire to do well, it is tempered by the knowledge that golf has changed – particularly since, I would say, the middle of 1999.

At my age, 48, I have to look to the Senior Tour because it's tough out on the main Tour. I thought at one point I wouldn't really want to drag myself away from where I had spent all my professional life, but that was about three years ago, and since then things have changed. Technology has accelerated and it is putting the game into the hands of the younger guys. They hit so hard and high, and of course the course designers these days are very much playing into their hands by building courses longer under the misconception that that makes it harder for the longer hitters. In fact, if I were taking on Tiger Woods, I would much rather it was at Sunningdale than Firestone.

My return to the professional world of golf came, as I've mentioned, courtesy of the Beeb at the Benson & Hedges, but before I was allowed on the Belfry course I had to go through a little tutorial along with another first-timer, Andy Cotter, who had previously worked in radio. We were taken out with Ken Brown to become accustomed to the on-course equipment. This was totally new to me because before I had just sat in a box watching the images and commentating; now we have to follow a group, go to where the ball finishes, assess the situation and get out of the way as quickly as possible. Our first couple of attempts were nothing less than complete bollocks, but we had to learn quickly.

I wandered around the course to see a few holes, then I went to say hello to Sam Torrance, joined another pro-am group and chatted to Colin Montgomerie. It was just nice to see the guys again and to feel that I was, in a way, back on Tour. I also drifted over to the Caddie Shack for a gourmet burger. It would have been rude not to. The whole experience felt a bit like going home, for I had spent the previous 25 years on Tour and I had an awful lot of friends there, so it was great to catch up with them again. The Shack is a good place to learn the news and enjoy a snack or two.

Being at the Belfry also gave me the opportunity to get reacquainted with my swing, and I was given permission to use the range after play on Thursday and Friday. I had been hitting balls for a couple of weeks, but this was a chance to see my new coach Pete Cowen for a couple of good sessions. The longest I had ever gone without practice in my entire career was no more than two and a half months; this time I had gone a full seven without hitting a shot, and that was just an enormous length of time. Looking back, I should perhaps have stirred my stumps between chemo sessions and tried to hit a few balls, but to be honest I didn't have the energy or the desire. Anyway, my hat would have kept slipping off!

When I first went up to hit balls the results were unbelievable. I wasn't too ambitious, just hitting half sand wedges, but I hardly knew which end of the club to hold. I took a three-quarter swing and had to put my right foot forward straight after impact to prevent myself from falling over. That is no exaggeration – I really did nearly topple. It did become easier, but I was swinging very, very badly.

It was the first time I had seen Pete since late September 2000 at the German Masters. It was obvious that there was an awful lot of work to do, and he set me off in the right direction. The good thing about Pete is that I can understand what I'm working on. Only time will tell whether it really works, but I feel settled, as if I'm working on the same things pretty much all the time. The long-term goals are just to get rid of the quirky aspects of my swing, not necessarily to change it. Anyway, I felt it was a good start. I was hitting balls again and Pete was giving me a few pointers.

I was also able to socialise a bit that week. There was a dinner one night for the BBC. I had received an invitation a few weeks earlier, after I had agreed to do the commentary, from Lord Daresbury, who is head of the De Vere company, owners of the Belfry. I'm not a great one for big dinners, so I rang up Ken and asked him what it was all about. He said I would be all right, that it was just the BBC, Lord Daresbury and a couple of other people. He added that it would be very relaxed and that I would enjoy it. I asked him how I should address the good lord, and he replied, 'I call him Pete.'

The evening did indeed turn out to be pleasant and relaxing, which is more than I can say for my first stint of commentary. It wasn't too bad when I was in the booth because you can do your research and think of things to say, but it wasn't easy being out on the course because you have to improvise all the time. Quite often when they tell you to speak you might not have thought of anything interesting to say, or there might not be anything interesting to talk about. But the most difficult thing is actually to get a look at how the ball is sitting, then retreat to a point where you can talk without the player hearing you when he's over his shot. I was never too sure about this critical distance, and I did get far too near once and had to pretend to have gone technical. I was still within the player's earshot when the producer said, 'Come in, Mark, ready for you.' I just said nothing, so the producer told those in the box they couldn't get hold of me and to continue talking.

It took me a number of holes to get used to it, but eventually I sort of got the hang of things. It was still bloody hard work, though. You have to dash off up the fairway to see the ball's lie, get to a safe place, then dash up to the green to have a look at their putts, then shoot off out of the way again so you can talk. Then, as soon as they have putted, you have to get up to the next hole and then get out of the way again. You're always a third of a hole ahead and rushing off, so it's not easy. Fortunately, the hours weren't too long because we were only on in the afternoon, so it was relatively short and sweet.

I did the Open later in the year, and that was 9.30 a.m. until seven at night. That is much harder, but it was great fun because I enjoyed working with Ken and former US PGA champion Wayne Grady. Peter Alliss and Alex Hay were also nothing short of brilliant to work with, both so professional. Peter really is the master of the art, and watching him in action was inspiring as well as educational.

One of the things commentary work for the BBC allowed me to do was take a close look at one or two of the new kids on the tee. Sweden's Henrik Stenson in particular stood out at the Belfry, and not simply because he held his nerve to win the tournament. He had a known pedigree having won the Challenge Tour money list the previous season, and what I saw of him at the Belfry was extremely impressive. It is no exaggeration on my part to say that he played magnificently because I watched every shot. Afterwards, BBC frontman Steve Rider asked me on air if Stenson had what it took to be a Ryder Cup player. I said, 'Absolutely.' It was a statement that would perfectly outline the vagaries of golf, because just a short time after doing so well, Henrik could hardly hit a fairway. He was in real trouble with his game and didn't really know what to do about it. Although in his case I'm sure there will be far more days when he will hit the middle of the fairway rather than the centre of an oak tree, it just shows that in golf as in life you simply don't know what's around the corner.

4. PLAYING BY THE RULES

Having reacquainted myself with the game and the practice range, the time was fast approaching when I would have to start earning a crust again, although I knew that whatever crumbs came my way would not make much of a meal. I was certainly not expecting to start shooting in the low 60s (not that I ever did).

Wentworth, which meanders wonderfully through a delightful stretch of the Surrey countryside, is a course where I have played reasonably well over the years, although generally when it wasn't very hard and bouncy which, unfortunately for me, it was at the 2001 Volvo PGA. I didn't feel confident going on to the Burma Road. It was playing very short, which wouldn't have been so bad had the greens been holding, but they were like concrete which immediately favoured those with a hot short game. Mine had warmed up to ice cold during my practice sessions in Yorkshire – a fact outlined in my warm-up round with Sam Torrance and two other good friends, Ross McFarlane and Gordon J. Brand, who no longer played on the Tour but had qualified from the Northern Order of Merit. It felt great to be back on the course in such company, though not that enjoyable when Gordon birdied the last to give him and Sam victory which, like telling me the result of a Grand Prix as I was watching the final laps, was typical of Gordon. His youngest daughter is no better. My first round of golf after my illness was against 13-year-old Lizzie – she beat me as well.

Furthermore, I handed Sam £20, which is my maximum. Parting with my hard-earned is an act I do not relish in the least, and playing against Sam can be fraught with danger because he normally has more bets running than a busy bookmaker's on a Saturday afternoon. I don't mind the odd pound here and there, but with Sam you never really know where you stand. You can win the match and the bye and the bye-bye and 30 seconds later you're handing him a cheque for six grand. He is an absolute nightmare to bet with, so giving him £20 felt like I was £5,980 up, while he probably felt as if I'd ripped him off because he knows I'm an easy touch in gambling matters. In fact, I don't like gambling at all. As my former coach Gavin Christie used to say, there is nothing wrong with a small bet, but not a gamble.

It was nice to hear from Gavin – nicknamed 'The Rhino' because he is thick-skinned and charges a lot – on a couple of occasions during my illness because we had split earlier in the season after 35 years together. The parting was not terribly acrimonious, but we had had a fair old difference of opinion in April 2000 over my failure to play in the Seve Ballesteros Trophy – a decision he had considered the wrong one. He is still doing a bit of teaching at St Andrews and probably spending no more than 70p a month on personal expenses. Now I was in the very capable hands of Pete Cowen, who had given my game a badly needed once-over before my return.

I was out with Ross again for the first two rounds at Wentworth, along with one of the new youngsters, Van Phillips. It was great not to have a superstar draw, as we call being paired with the big names, and to be able to feel my way back into the routine of Tour golf without too much attention. The crowd had been great in terms of welcoming me back, although I did find it amusing when one chap said, 'Great to see you back, Mark, we thought we'd lost you in the winter.' I had also seen Nick Faldo to thank him for his get-well card, and I wished him good luck for the year. We may have had our differences, but I don't bear any animosity towards him. As far as I was concerned, the events of the previous year were over and done with, and certainly overshadowed by events in the winter. In any case, I'm not one to hold grudges.

The crowd were great on the tee and I was actually a bit edgy as I prepared for my first swing, not because I was emotional, but because I thought I might hit the ball sideways and hurt someone. I sort of scooped it away semi-efficiently, but my game was, to be honest, nothing short of pathetic and I missed the cut comprehensively without breaking sweat. It was probably no more or less than I should have expected, but still disappointing because I hadn't lived up to my own prediction. I thought I would miss the cut by seven, but I went out much more comfortably than that. At least I was back.

Woburn between 31 May and 3 June was the next stop, and, if nothing else, I knew I was in for a few tasty dinners with the Browns, Ken and Dawn, who live close to the course and are extremely good hosts. I played a lot better that week; in fact, my game would sort of settle down into a pattern between Woburn and the Dutch Open at the end of July, but I carried on putting very, very poorly, and that was going to stop me doing well. I started putting a wee bit better only around the end of August during the Scottish PGA, and then made six cuts out of seven. Only then did I really feel as if I was back on Tour. I had the chance to do all right, but I wasn't sure when it was going to happen. At least my game looked as though it was capable of performing. The thing is, scoring in general is so low these days that if you don't putt at least reasonably well you might as well leave the clubs in the boot of the car and head for McDonald's.

One odd thing about this comeback period was the total absence of hay fever. I wondered if the rigours of the winter had cleansed me of my weakness when it came to pollen. I asked my consultant about it later in the year and he explained that because the chemo affects the immune system, it no longer reacted to the presence of pollen. I was most disappointed to learn that as my body recovers I can apparently look forward to fits of sneezing again.

Missing qualification for the Open in July, while a big disappointment, at least gave me the chance to hook up with the BBC again. They had a decent-sized team for the tournament, including Peter Alliss, Alex Hay, Ken Brown, Wayne Grady, Julian Tutt, Mike Hughesden, Laura Davies and myself. Part of the preliminaries was a meeting with R&A officials for a run through the rules to give the commentators some idea of what was happening. As usual with the rules they can be incredibly complicated, mainly comprising exactly what the players have to do if the ball ends up against grandstands or metal fencing. Metal fencing is quite often a real killer because you are never allowed to move it. If you're outside it but within so many club lengths, you can drop your ball inside; if not, you drop it outside, but of course that depends on which club you use, not only for the shot but for measuring distances. It does get very confusing. Inside, outside, upside, down-side – you often wonder which side you are on, but they told us where the marshals would be and how many rules officials would be on the course. I asked if either the marshals or rules officials were given any form of competency test, but they didn't seem all that amused and the answer was negative.

The rules of golf are incredibly complex and plentiful and provoke debate, argument and controversy at whatever level the game is played. New issues crop up all the time, but few anecdotes can compare to that which featured one of Britain's best ever caddies, Dave Musgrove, who was with Sandy Lyle when he won his majors, American Lee Janzen and several other top-drawer golfers. He was involved in one of the most unusual rules stories I have ever heard.

Janzen had taken his approach putt on one hole, marked his ball, then thrown it to Mussy to clean. The ball disappeared in the sun, Mussy missed it, and after hitting his hand it bounced away, but to where nobody actually knew. When Mussy got his eyesight back after staring into the sun, it was nowhere to be found. They were sure it had not rolled off the green, and after discussion with the other players they decided it must have ended up in the bottom pocket of the golf bag which was propped open by an energy drink. The pocket was full of balls with exactly the same markings, several of them with exactly the same number, so they got them all out and on one of them there was a small piece of grass. That was how they identified the ball that had been thrown to Mussy, otherwise it would have been a two-shot penalty for Janzen and a frosty next few holes for the pair of them.

Players are always throwing the ball to caddies and occasionally it ends up going into a lake. If they don't get it out, it's an extra two shots on the card. It happened to Scotland's Raymond Russell early in 2001 at the Forest of Arden. His caddie went wading into the lake but just could not find the ball.

Just because a player has been on Tour for a long time does not seem to help, as I demonstrated to my cost in Belgium a couple of years ago. I was standing on a sprinkler right by the green, so I took my nearest point, measured a club length and dropped the ball, not nearer the hole. It was on the apron, as it had been originally. I obviously gained no advantage and two-putted for my par. Someone had seen me on the television or something like that and it was reported to the tournament director, no less an intimidating figure than Andy McFee, one of the most stringent rules officials to be found anywhere in the game. I had been warned that there might be a problem on completion of the hole, and when I arrived on the next tee, looming large was the aforementioned McFee. He told me that I had breached Rule 186(F), or some such number, that it was a minor rather than major breach and punishable by a two-stroke penalty. I should have just dropped it at the nearest point and not taken the extra club length. I have not done it since, but I should have known better. I had been on Tour long enough to know and there was no excuse. It was annoying because I was on the leaderboard at the time, and my descent from that moment was predictable.

Something similar happened to Sergio Garcia in Australia at the start of 2001 when the young Spaniard took a line-of-sight ruling from a hoarding. Sergio's first mistake was to confer with playing partner Greg Norman, whose knowledge of the rules, like that of so many others, including my own, does not qualify him for a seat on *Mastermind*. The Great White Shark was not that great in the circumstances; Sergio would have been better advised to send for a referee there and then, but the pair of them opted for their own interpretation. Sergio measured out the first club length, and knew that he could drop the ball up to another club's length away. Although he dropped the ball no closer to the hole, it rolled back into the first club length and that was where he transgressed the rules. He played it from where it was, thinking that he was perfectly entitled to, because it gave him a better second shot, but it was from the wrong place and he suffered a two-shot penalty after a later, on-site consultation with John Paramor.

To say Garcia went ballistic is to understate what happened when the ruling went against him, but he was messing with the wrong guy with Paramor, one of the world's foremost rules authorities and somebody who is immovable when he knows the good book is on his side. Garcia, who was leading the tournament at the time, sounded off to Paramor and anybody else within hearing distance. There was quite a song and dance about everything and the Spaniard was fined a fairly significant sum by the Tournament Committee. He had no defence because what he had said about the official was quite wrong.

Sergio is not the first and won't be the last Spaniard – and it wouldn't matter if he were Swedish, Swiss or Sowetan – to find Paramor unbudgeable, and quite rightly so. Ask Seve Ballesteros, whose ball ended among the roots of a tree and directly behind it on the last hole at Valderrama during one Volvo Masters there. Seve, like all professionals never slow to use the rules to his advantage, tried to get a free drop from an animal scrape. He and Paramor stood there inspecting the ball, the site and the predicament for an age, but the official was convinced that Seve should not get a free drop under the circumstances. There would be only one winner.

Seve was also the unwitting victim of one of his own adjudications during an exhibition match or pre-tournament shootout with Zimbabwean Tony Johnstone, or 'Ovies' as we call him. He earned the nickname as a kid. Apparently, when he was less than satisfied with a tee shot he always wanted to hit over again, and the sobriquet stuck. Anyway, the pair had driven over the brow of a hill, then Seve gave a quick interview by the tee. By the time he rejoined his playing partner, Ovies was standing in the right rough addressing the ball close to a tree. He was doing it with a very exaggerated stance, with one foot drawn so far back it caught a sprinkler. He asked Seve if he could get a drop and was told no, because he was not taking a proper stance. Ovies tried it from another angle and with another unlikely gait, but again Seve refused to let him take relief. 'Well, it's a pity there's no free drop, Seve,' Ovies remarked, 'because this is your ball.'

Rules officials are not the most popular people in golf. Their standing in a player's eye is often determined by the nature of the ruling, but they don't always win the battle, as happened once in Cannes. Mark Roe's ball finished close to a drain and he believed he was entitled to relief. A French referee said he was not, and reiterated the sentiment when asked to reconsider. After ten minutes' debate, Roey asked for a second opinion and was turned down, to which he said, 'I'm going to sit on my bag and wave every group through until I get a second opinion.' Eventually, the referee drove back to the clubhouse, handed in his radio, keys to the buggy, coat and badges and told mystified officials, 'I cannot take any more.' He was not seen again that week.

Another interesting story, although possibly embroidered, was told to me by former Tour colleague now television commentator Robert Lee about a friend of his called Julian Cotton, who was invited to a corporate event in America. On the first tee he was flattered to be presented with a box of balls all of which had his name printed on them. Halfway through the round he hit a shot on to an adjoining fairway, but by the time he reached it he found the lady captain addressing it with a fairway wood. 'Excuse me, madam,' he said, 'but I think that could be my ball,' at which she bent over, picked it up, inspected it and replied, 'I don't think so, I always play Julian Cottons.'

We have all had our scrapes with officialdom and the rules at some point in our careers. I remember playing in the Walker Cup at St Andrews and on one hole my ball finished on a road with a stone lodged right behind it. I called a referee to ask if I could move the stone and he said not if it was solidly embedded. I flicked it out with a tee peg and said, 'It's not, look.' He just said, 'If you do that again, I will give the hole to the Americans.' It is difficult to award holes willy-nilly, but I should not have not done that really, although I was not very old at the time (as if that's much of a defence).

Fortunately, I was not involved in any rulings in 2001 at Royal Lytham as I commentated both on the course and in the box for the first couple of days. The on-course work was totally different to what I had experienced at the Belfry, where I had an assistant to hold my microphone, battery pack and everything else. There, I just wandered around eating burgers, apples and sweets, and when they came to me I grabbed the microphone and spoke into it. At the Open, we had our own packs and they taught us how to change batteries when we needed to, which for somebody as non-technical as me was vitally important. Fortunately, the producers were not coming to us for advice on putts at the Open, and that made it easier because we could just stay ahead of the game. We didn't have to hang around and look at the lines, which to be honest is not easy when you aren't on the green (it can be just as hard when you are).

The first day went pretty well. I was not too bad in the box and OK on the course, and I finished the day believing I had handled myself reasonably satisfactorily. It was a feeling that came to an abrupt halt the following day with one of those experiences I had been warned about – a day when there wasn't much of interest happening and consequently I couldn't think of anything to say. I had also been told that there would be occasions when I would be having a break, something unusual would happen and somebody else would have the joy of commentating on it.

Things did not improve when I went out on the course in the afternoon. I was sent to watch Paul Lawrie, but as soon as I joined him he bogeyed and dropped out of the picture, so I was shunted off to somebody else. I caught up with David Duval at the ninth and watched him hit his tee shot on the next straight into the right-hand fairway bunker. I said into the mike to the producer, 'I've got Duval here, I think he's sizing up to have a go at it and it has got double bogey written all over it.' Something was happening elsewhere so they couldn't come to me, and sure enough Duval went for it, hit the top of the bunker, left it in and double-bogeyed. So he too slipped off the board and I was despatched elsewhere. In fact, I spent the whole afternoon wandering around not doing anything. You get days when you feel like that when you're playing the game, so I guess it's the same when commentating.

The weekend action, though, was extremely good, particularly on the Saturday. It was probably one of the most exciting day's golf I had seen and it was a privilege to commentate on it. Peter, Alex, Ken and Wayne were so easy to work with, and that made a big difference. Not only were they very accommodating to a newcomer, they were also bloody good at their jobs.

And Lytham was set up magnificently in 2001, perfect for the world's premier golfing event. I don't think they could have prepared that course better. It was a perfect combination of width of fairways, length of rough and pace and quality of greens. It should be used as a model for future Opens. Everyone who knows Lytham knew that it would be the one course where Tiger Woods would not have a big advantage because of the distances he hits, as there are relatively few holes where you can carry all the trouble. Tiger could not tame it, and I was delighted to see Duval win. The American had been a tremendous player for several years, and if anyone deserved a major it was him. He played magnificently through the last two days.

It was also good to see Darren Clarke up there challenging, because of the current crop of British players I think he is the man most likely to win an Open. Admittedly I haven't seen much of the new young players under links conditions, but Darren is long and straight and controls the ball very well in the wind. I'm convinced he will be a big contender in Opens over the next few years. I just hope he has as much pleasure playing in them as I have experienced throughout my long career.

5. EARLY DAYS

Although I was born in Manchester, I remember little of my time there – not surprising, considering that I wasn't as tall as a short putter when the family left. We moved south to Slough, then north to Melton Mowbray where my dad, who had had fairly humble beginnings, worked his way up to managing director with Pedigree Pet Foods. They were part of the Mars Group – a real bonus, particularly at Christmas, because we were never short of chocolates. Basically mine was a very happy childhood alongside my sister Helen, who is eighteen months younger, and brother Richard, ten years my junior, although I did suffer more than my fair share of illnesses, the worst of which was TB when I was ten.

It was while we were in Melton Mowbray that I first got a taste of the sport that would become a major part of my life. I started to caddie occasionally for my dad and played a few times before we moved to Uffington, close to Stamford in Lincolnshire. The bug was firmly implanted in my system. My dad joined Burghley Park, the club within the grounds of Burghley House at Stamford, and it was there that I was to spend the majority of my amateur career after I started playing regularly at the age of twelve. That was about the first time I was strong enough to wield a club properly since my bout with TB. I was still pretty weedy when I started playing regularly and didn't exactly get the ball 'out there' until I was about eighteen, but I became pretty keen straight away, like kids do when they get their teeth into something. Mine were embedded.

The professional at Burghley Park was none other than Gavin Christie, a straight-talking, no-nonsense Scot who had a canny knack of identifying flaws and eradicating them. I became his pupil, and our relationship lasted for 35 years. There was a heck of a crop of juniors at the club. At least six, maybe seven of us had a handicap of four or less by the age of sixteen – no mean achievement in those days, or any other for that matter. I think only one, perhaps two of the others – Graham Cowley definitely – ended up turning pro, but a couple went on to be Cambridge Blues and we regularly supplied three-quarters of the county junior side and a good number for the senior one. All the rest reached good amateur standards, but ended up doing other things. It was great to be involved at that time at Burghley Park with the other good young players because we pushed one another along, bringing out the best in ourselves and generally revelling in the fierce but fair competition that existed.

A picture of Jack Nicklaus may appear on the first of my scrapbooks, but I didn't have any particular boyhood idols. However, I did spend a lot of time studying the top players without trying to model myself on them. It has always been difficult for me to decode other people's methods and adapt them to my own style. I always seemed to have a natural sense of timing, although it was not always obvious through my short, lashing swing.

I considered myself fairly well balanced when I was twelve. I was shy and not a great communicator, but that is a fairly normal trait in kids up to about sixteen years of age. I just wanted to play golf first, second and third. I found myself on a steady improvement curve through my teens up to when I turned professional. Burghley was a great place to be based and the members were all keen on playing in syndicates in the week. We all put a ball in and the best score took the lot. That really got the competitive juices flowing and we did it week in, week out when I was at home.

Practice was not something I did a great deal of in the early days, but as my accumulation of balls increased so did my sessions off the course. They intensified as my handicap lowered, and by the time I reached scratch at eighteen I was averaging about five hours plus at least one round of golf a day.

Many of the older members at Burghley were brilliant with the younger ones, particularly Howard Mulligan and Les Pepper. Howard used to take us all over the place to play golf, and Les, who had strong ties and contacts throughout the game, was always on hand to ferry us to county matches. I cannot thank them enough for what they did for us all. Les got an award a couple of years ago from the English Golf Union in recognition of his services to golf, and Howard is now secretary at Burghley, and I'm sure all the juniors around at that time remember their help. You don't think about it when you're a kid because you're too wrapped up in your own little world, blinkered to everything else, but when you look back years later you reflect on just how much thought they put in and time they spared us. They didn't have to do it, but they did, and it made a big difference.

I was a reasonable performer at school, getting nine O levels and a couple of A levels. I took only two As because of the way the syllabus was structured. For some reason I couldn't do Maths, French and Economics, I could do only two of them, so I chose Maths and Economics, which is pathetic really, but it didn't bother me at the time. Although I have had little cause to use them, I have never been disqualified for adding my score up wrongly. My dad had asked me to stay on and get my A levels, then I could play amateur golf and see how things developed. That is exactly what I did, although I must admit my enthusiasm for my studies did not match that for golf. All I was interested in was getting the homework out of the way so that I could get out on the course.

It was, at this stage, my hope to make a living out of playing the game because I dreaded the thought of office life. As long as I could scrape through with enough money to exist on, I would be happy. I worked in a warehouse in the winter and did bits and bobs – decorating, some bar work at the golf club – to try to support myself on the amateur circuit. I didn't know anyone on the road, so to combat the boredom and loneliness I invariably headed to the practice area. It was a blessing, because it meant my game improved considerably.

I will never forget my first amateur 'cheque', or voucher as it was, at the Burghley Park auction meeting because it was for the princely sum of £20, which in 1968 was a significant amount for me and, I guess, a lot of others. It was also a profitable day for my dad: he had not only purchased me in the auction, but also the outright winner, whose 66–68 net eclipsed my 72–65. Still, it was no disgrace to finish second to one Palmer, though not the legendary one.

Looking back, it appears that I was already in training for a strained relationship with the press because few photographers, if any, managed to get me to say 'cheese' and I often found it difficult to stare into the lens. I remember golf writer Gordon Richardson once reporting that he had been warned that interviewing me was a bit like trying to prise atomic secrets out of a Russian spy, but he went on to add: 'Different, Mark James certainly is. Introspective, determined, restlessly dissatisfied with second-best, level-headed, shrewd, serious, soft-spoken, even shy.' I recognise a few of those traits, but whatever people's feelings – and I could never really figure out why people were particularly interested in me – these were very happy times on the course, ones I will always remember fondly.

I was always particularly pleased to hear people talk in praise of Les Pepper because he really did throw himself into the club. I'm sure it was his work as chairman of the greens committee that helped me collect the club's Coronation Cup as a fifteen-year-old. If there was a pivotal moment in my early amateur career it was that success, shooting a gross 77 off a handicap of thirteen. It was the first round of my life I played almost mistake-free, and it was an incredible feeling to play an entire eighteen holes without hitting a particularly bad shot. They were not necessarily all perfect shots because I did not hit a long way at that age, but it was a huge round for me because it was as if a barrier had been broken. It left an imprint on me because it was my first taste of realising that a golfer could have a round without making any serious errors and could play believing that every shot was going to be a good one.

Another of the peaks in my early amateur career at Burghley was when I became junior champion in 1970 with a net score of 67 off five. It was at about this time that the local press were starting to suggest that the club was producing the Tony Jacklins of the future, but I never looked much further than the next shot, knowing that if I was ever to walk the same fairways as the British and US champion a million and more practice balls would have to be hit on the practice range.

There were several of us from the club representing Lincolnshire in the early 1970s. I made my debut against Norfolk on 9 May 1971, although I cannot for the life of me remember the result. What I do know was that it was about that time that Gavin Christie left the club to take up a similar position in Scotland, although our teacher–pupil relationship would continue for many a year afterwards. His good work at the club was confirmed by the honours board through the number of youngsters he had coached to county standard and beyond.

Having been runner-up to club mate John Cross in 1970, I was very proud to go one better the following year to retain the Lincolnshire Junior Trophy and break the course record at Sleaford at the same time. My progress was such that in August 1971 I was nominated by the county to join up with the British Boys and enter the trials to get into the team. Some were already qualified automatically, but other spots were available through trials.

I had never travelled anywhere of any distance before, although I was always being ferried around by either my dad, Les Pepper or Howard Mulligan to local events. This event was in Berwick, but I had passed my driver's test a couple of months before so I dragged myself out of bed at about lunchtime, as you do at that age, borrowed my mum's Volkswagen Beetle and headed up the A1 to Scotch Corner and a whole new world. Driving that Beetle was a wonderful experience. It rattled on down hills at 85mph, but chugged up them at about 45, and the heating did not work which was a bit of a pain because the weather was horrendous and the journey seemed to take an eternity. It got to about ten at night and I was still going across from Scotch Corner, so I decided I had better stop somewhere for the night. I knocked on the door of a bed and breakfast establishment and asked if they could accommodate me. The lady said, 'Yep, follow me,' and took me upstairs to this enormous room where there were no fewer than 30 beds. I had never seen anything like it before or since, and when I asked which one I should take she just replied, 'You can take the lot, we're not busy.' I was the only person in there, and I spent the night wondering if Peter Cushing or Vincent Price might suddenly appear at a window.

The next day I parted with a one-pound note and set off again on my journey into the unknown. I had absolutely no idea what to expect because I was just a boy from the backwoods. I must have looked like something from an Oxfam shop when I arrived in Berwick with my small carry bag and a Goudie driver which had a dent in the grip where I had shanked a ball on the practice ground into it. I don't believe I had the maximum permitted fourteen clubs, and I only used the driver on special occasions because I rarely got the ball airborne with it. To put it mildly, I was not quite like some of the others who were likely to be in the team. Anyway, I got up there for a practice round and some of the names were already there – the likes of Pip Elson and Howard Clark wandering around with their enormous sponsored golf bags and huge head covers bigger than a Labrador. They were all smoking eight-inch-long cigarettes and generally exuding an air of being about ten years older than me. Nobody was more shocked than me when I went out and shot 70 and 74 in qualifying. I think I finished second. I definitely got picked for the team to play Scotland, which was an amazing surprise to me and probably many others.

The records show that I played with D.J. Warr – I think his name was Dave, but I'm not sure because I'm convinced I partnered somebody else. What I'm more certain about is that I was way out of my depth. It was to our surprise and not as a result of the quality of our play that we halved our foursomes match with R.G. Cairns and C.H. Bloice. (It seemed as though people had no Christian names in those days. I always remember P.B.H. May playing cricket for England and F.S. Trueman bowling.) I was just pleased to be back in the sanctuary of the clubhouse, but even there I was not immune from having my central nervous system attacked. For reasons unclear to me, and probably to them as well, the England powers-that-be put me at nine in a ten-man team for the afternoon singles. My initial feelings would unfortunately come true: on seeing the batting order, I just thought, 'Oh my God, I hope it doesn't come down to me.' They put all the superstars like Elson, Clark and Peter Deeble out first and loaded the bottom end with the 'choppers'. Bobby Davro's brother and fellow surprise David Nankeville was off after me in tenth place. We were the unlikeliest members of the team and they had put us in the hot seat. How would I react if it came down to me? In all probability I would be looking for the nearest point of relief.

So far I had been relatively low profile, keeping out of everybody's way and avoiding offending R&A members, that sort of thing. We headed off in the afternoon and before long the horror of horrors scenario developed. It was obvious the match was going to be tight and it was becoming increasingly clear that I was going to play an unwanted and unavoidably pivotal part in the outcome. Come the seventeenth and my match against the aforementioned Bloice was the only one left on the course. We were one point behind and I was one up, and all the officials streamed out on to the course to watch. There were people in jackets and ties everywhere, just the sort of people I didn't get on with. I'm not much better at it these days, but then I was disastrous in their company. I just couldn't understand what they were saying half the time because they had 'plummy' accents and they were all holding pink gins and waffling. 'Who is this fellow James? My God, look at his trousers, they're a bit short, aren't they?' I was wishing I was at home watching *Star Trek* or *Mission Impossible*, or even peeling the potatoes.

Quite a crowd gathered, including all the other players, which was an embarrassment because they all knew some of us were choppers even if the suits did not. We both drove into the right rough. Cecil (for that was Bloice's Christian name) played his second shot first and shanked it over the railway line. He could have shaken hands there and then, but he must have known I was just as unpredictable as he was. He played another and hit it up just left of the green for four. I then hit my second with a nine-iron into a greenside bunker, but still no great panic because I was one up and just needed to get it out and two-putt. Everything was looking hunky-dory, and I was starting to smile and wave to the crowd. Even the jacketed ones were giving me the odd nod of encouragement.

I settled in the bunker and promptly shanked the ball. It shot right over the back of the green, down a bank and back up the other side. I now had a hideous chip for my fourth shot. I tried to bump it into the bank and up on to the green, but it stuck in the bank. Both Cecil and I had now had four, and I was not in good shape at all. I was certainly a bit nervous, and the throng of officials were now spluttering in their pink gins. Instead of nodding their heads they were shaking them, and it all became hugely embarrassing.

I decided I had better hit my trusty sand wedge off the back foot, so I gave the ball a chop, thinned it and watched it hurtle across the green towards obscurity. I'm not sure which county it would have stopped in had it not hit the pin flush in the centre of the stick and come to rest no more than a foot away from the hole. Cecil then chipped to two feet, and now we had both played five. He missed from two feet and I knocked mine in to win the hole with a six to a seven, and England halved the entire match. I may have saved the team from defeat, but I was as red as a postbox.

I doubt I was the hero of the hour. I certainly cannot remember being so because I probably just slunk off and fainted under a bush somewhere, or went back to practise. But that was my introduction to international golf. It was a strange affair, largely memorable for my never having seen so many people watching me play before. What I do remember vividly is buying some fish and chips, eating them in the car and thinking, 'My God, I don't want to be in that situation again.'

I stayed on for the British Boys trials and lost by one hole in the fourth round to somebody called T.P. Gifford. We played reasonably early, and afterwards I decided I would return to the links to have a look at a superstar. I studied the draw and noticed that Howard Clark was somewhere near the back nine. 'He is supposed to be very good,' I thought to myself, 'so I'll have a look.' At the age of just seventeen Howard had arms like my legs, and he used to hit the ball absolutely miles. I caught up with him on the fourteenth or fifteenth, a 170-yard par three on the back nine which I could remember hitting a five-iron to. Howard stood on the tee and rolled up his sleeves; I could see all his muscles rippling as he took out an eight-iron. Obviously Howard must have had contacts in the Titleist factory or somewhere because he took out a new ball (I think I used just the one the entire week), teed it up and gave it the most enormous smack. The ball soared into the afternoon sky and was close to orbit before it plummeted to earth, straight into the hole. That was the first shot I ever saw Howard hit, and I walked away thinking, 'Jesus, I have a lot of practising to do.'

I have never really enjoyed practising an awful lot, but it was something that had to be done. Most parts of playing golf are reasonably enjoyable, so you put up with the practising. I wouldn't say that I disliked it, but I never found it overly thrilling; it was certainly always a distant second to actually playing the game. However, I did work very hard at my game. I knew it was the only way to improve, so I went out and did it.

After that eye-opener in and against Scotland, my career graph showed a steady if unspectacular improvement. In May 1972 the local paper announced that I had 'rocketed to fame' and put Burghley 'firmly on the map' by finishing third in the English Amateur Open Stroke Play Champion-ship for the Brabazon Trophy. I was still at school at the time so it was a particularly impressive achievement. It was a bonus having dad as the club captain that year, although the national press's penchant for exaggeration saw them tag me as 'prodigiously talented', especially since I had gone there hoping for nothing more than a top-twenty finish. Les Pepper was quoted as saying that I must be Lincolnshire's best golfer and that my performance was a great thing for me, club and county. Dad must have been proud too because he went into print saying, 'We would have been delighted had he finished anywhere in the top ten.'

I left formal education in the summer of 1972 and went full time on the amateur circuit. One of my dad's friends, Tom Regis, gave me a job in his Sally Morlands supermarket warehouse. For a few months I humped stuff around, hopefully trying to build up my muscles because I was a seven-stone weakling who used to get sand kicked in his face in bunkers, so much so that I had to buy a pair of Ken Brown sand goggles. I worked there for the next few winters and also did a bit of decorating here and there and some bar work at the golf club. I generally did my best to support myself, but obviously dad had to give me a few bob.

The highlight of what was a very short career at that time came in 1973 when rounds of 71 and 73 at Glasgow Gailes were good enough to get me into the Open at Royal Troon. A photographer even got a rare snap of me with a smile on my face, though it was only a half one. It was an unbelievable experience, and although I shot 83 in the first round it was only four more than my playing partner, former US Open champion Ken Venturi. My mum ventured into print after the first round when she told a reporter, 'I think he must have been a little disappointed because he did not ring last night.' I doubt that I rang the following night either because I shot a second-round 85 and, overcome by teenage depression, described the championship as a 'disastrous tournament for me', albeit an experience that would not stop me trying to qualify the next year. It was the size and nature of the crowd that really surprised me. They reacted enthusiastically to every good shot, although after returning 83 and 85 I didn't leave Royal Troon with much applause ringing in my ears.

The experience did not dull my appetite for the game whatsoever, for Tom Weiskopf was not the only golfer to win an Open that weekend. At exactly the same time as the American was holing the winning putt on the west coast of Scotland, I was signing for the lowest round at the Peterborough Standard Open. The real Open had not seen the last of me as an amateur: I would go one better the following year at Royal Lytham by playing three rounds.

If I had a stellar season in the amateur game it would be 1974 when, at the age of twenty, I won the English Amateur at Woodhall Spa, beating no less a stalwart of the amateur game than (now Sir) Michael Bonallack along the way to a 6 & 5 triumph over East Herts' John Watts. I'm not sure I recognised myself in Pat Ward-Thomas's subsequent description, but he referred to my game as having a sound pattern and rhythm and thought my pitching revealed an excellence of striking. 'He was able to make the ball settle on the green softly and he putted beautifully, noticeably standing absolutely still as he did so,' he added. 'He showed no sign that impatience would betray him, although he remained a perfectionist, visibly dissatisfied with anything but the perfect stroke. This is an admirable trait, but one that could have its pitfalls.'

I received the trophy from another great ambassador for the amateur game, Neil Hotchkin, president of Woodhall Spa, and I even managed to smile for the official photograph. Along with the trophy he bestowed on me honorary membership, and I was able to practise on that wonderful turf they have there on many occasions while I lived fairly locally.

Also in 1974 I made the national side for the Home Internationals, which capped a very good year for me, particularly on the team front. Burghley won the Clubs' Championship in Lincolnshire, Lincolnshire won the English County Championship, and England won the Home Internationals. As a result I had every chance of making the Walker Cup team to face America the following May, because not much was going to happen or change between then and the time the team was picked.

It was an honour to make the team and a surprising experience, never more so than on the first morning when instead of the long lie-in I was expecting, the telephone rang in my bedroom at 7.15 – an unholy hour for anybody, particularly a 21-year-old. British team captain Dr David Marsh was on the line asking me to rise at once and play in the opening foursomes I had originally been left out of. First choice Peter Hedges had cut his head badly on a door the previous evening and needed three stitches in the wound. I had been put on stand-by, but I assumed Peter would recover. He didn't, and I was fortunate to partner Richard Eyles to the team's only foursomes victory on the first morning. One of our opponents was Jerry Pate, and I went on to beat the then US champion in the afternoon singles as well to cap a fine day's work. I wasn't quite sure, however, why the press, who had made much of my practising yoga, made me out to be a hero considering the team ended the first day 8–4 down against an American side containing, apart from Pate, Curtis Strange, Craig Stadler, Jay Haas, Gary Koch and George Burns.

We would finally succumb, for the twenty-second time in 25 attempts, 15½–18½, and I took little consolation from finishing as the team's top points scorer. On reflection, though, I suppose it should have been a satisfying performance.

6. PAY FOR PLAY

I had stayed amateur to play in the Walker Cup, but, looking back, in a way it was a waste of time because I didn't play particularly well for the rest of year after the match at St Andrews, although I did reach the final of the Amateur Championship immediately afterwards. I was bitterly disappointed to be beaten by American Vinny Giles at Hoylake, but I couldn't blame my hay fever (although I probably did at the time) because he was the better man on the day. After that it was just a question of waiting to turn professional. I was doing little more than treading water, and because of that I lost my focus along with my game to a certain extent.

I finally turned professional in October 1975, which now may seem a strange time to do it, but in those days it was just common sense. Players were only allowed to accept prize money after six months in the paid ranks, so since the tournaments started in April I had to make sure I left the amateur ranks more than six months before that to be eligible for money in European events when I started. It seems unbelievable looking back, but there must have been some reason for it at the time. For the life of me I cannot remember what it was, nor can I think what it might have been now.

My aims in professional golf were simple: to become the best golfer I could possibly be and to win as much money as possible. I gave myself five years to accomplish this because I wasn't prepared to forfeit my whole future to slogging away at the game. If I wasn't successful in that time then I would walk away and try to find something else to be good at. All I knew was that I was going to give it my best shot.

It was off to the African continent for my debut, carrying a head full of dreams and ambitions and a pocketful of my dad's money. He gave me a thousand pounds and told me, 'You had better make it last.' I think I told him I might be back for more in a fortnight. In all honesty, I didn't know if there was any more money where that came from, but I was lucky enough never to have to go back to him. In fact, I never paid him back. I hope he has forgotten about it because it will have accumulated quite a lot of interest by now.

My first tournament was in Glendower in South Africa at the end of October. There had been a match between Britain and the host nation just before the tournament and everybody seemed to be shooting 61 and 62. There were about eight different Hennings in the South African side and none of them shot more than 64. Even some of our guys were shooting really low, and I thought I was going to have my work cut out just to make the cut. I was not over confident, and my feelings of apprehension were far from soothed by what happened before I struck my first ever shot as a professional. I was in the semi rough, near the first tee, doing a few practice swings and I hit a stone with my driver. Much to my astonishment, half the insert dropped out and there was no chance to repair or replace it. It was not surprising that I shot 77–77 and missed the cut by a wide margin, having to hit every tee shot off the toe.

The experience, though, was wonderful because everybody seemed to be friendly. I had not socialised much on the amateur circuit – staying in really cheap B&Bs, I didn't get to know many of the players. It was slightly different among the pros, and I will never forget how helpful Harry Bannerman was in those early days, generally pointing the younger guys in the right direction. Not all the older guys were like that, but Harry was a scholar and a gentleman and I will always respect him for the help he gave me and other hopefuls who were out with the pros for the first time on that trip to South Africa.

I found my feet in Africa, moving on to Nigeria, Zambia and Kenya, and I also came across Ken Brown for the first time. We quickly discovered that we had the same aim in professional life: to become good golfers and annoy people. We were definitely successful in one of those departments. We didn't go out of our way to antagonise anybody, but we found it incredibly easy once we got the hang of it. It was like falling off a log, and when we fell off it was invariably into trouble. It took a monumental effort to turn the tide. Eventually, after a few years of just getting into trouble at every opportunity you start to expect it and almost look for it. I think then we both realised something had to change because clashing too often with authority gets a bit wearing. It has to be said that we did have an awful lot of bad luck as well, but it was no coincidence that our attitude switch came after we met the girlfriends who would become our respective wives.

Ken and I shared a passion for practice, although passion may be too strong a word in my case because it was not something I did for the pure love of it. We realised we would have to do plenty of it if we were ever to be as good or as well off financially as we wanted to be. There were relatively few European players who practised for as many hours in the 1970s as Ken and myself, maybe only Nick Faldo and Greg Norman when he came from Australia to join the Tour. We would willingly practise all day and then have dinner before going back out to the range and putting green for another couple of hours. That was standard, and it was probably easier to do then because I think there were fewer than twenty tournaments on the schedule so you could generally be more intense at those events.

Ken and I shared something else: attitude. I think we probably suffered from a terminal case of treating people and events as we found them, and that probably does not go down well in all walks of life. What people felt about us did not occupy much if any of our thinking. All we cared about was golf. Although girlfriends were starting to appear during the 1970s, Jane in my case and Dawn in Ken's were both working while we were away a lot of the time. Ken and I had pretty much the same habits and he was an ideal room mate. He did not snore, slept for eight hours a night without making any noise at all and was meticulous in matters of personal hygiene.

My golf improved steadily on the Safari Circuit and I soon found myself with more money than I'd started out with. I returned home early in 1976 having won £2,300 from nine events and then headed off towards Europe and some bigger purses en route to Royal Birkdale and the Open.

Birkdale, Turnberry and Royal St George's are probably my three favourites of all the Open courses, the first of these without doubt having the toughest start. The first hole at Birkdale is brutal: it looks as though you have to land the ball on to a saucer off the tee. The gap in the fairway is very narrow and the ball never quite seems to come off the left-hand humps, instead just getting caught in them. I remember it was particularly dry on the first day in 1976 and they had put the pin on a little knob. Every man and his dog was three-putting it. The course meanders wonderfully, though, and each hole seems to be well defined and designed, culminating in a really sporty finishing stretch. It seems the architect was looking to reward good play and penalise errant shots, so over the last four holes – although not particularly the last – you can shoot high or low and there are a couple of eagle chances. The last is a very tough par four, so the closing quartet makes, for me, the best finishing spread of any of the Open courses.

I started playing steadily on the European circuit – no spectacular fireworks, just picking up fairly regular cheques for learning my trade, as it were, until the Open at Royal Birkdale. I was playing reasonably well, but had no real reason to expect anything special, particularly after shooting a 76 in the first round and following it with a regulation 72. The weather was not all that good over the weekend; a blustery wind meant that scoring was not particularly easy. Entering the last round, I was in twenty-sixth place – not that anybody was all that interested in me, or had any reason to be. The world of golf was being shaken awake by the more startling talent of a young Spaniard called Severiano Ballesteros, who led by two going into the final round of only his second Open.

Seve would be denied by Johnny Miller, but I only had eyes for the little brown envelope which was thrust into my hands afterwards. It contained a cheque for £2,820, the prize for finishing in a tie for fifth, and wealth beyond my comprehension. Just where that record last-round 66 came from in those conditions I was not altogether sure, but the money was more than I imagined you could ever make in a week. With a good dose of luck stirred in every now and then, I have never really struggled financially since. I have not had too many slumps – well, the worst ones have not been so bad that I've had to consider selling the house, put it that way.

I remember coming away from the presentation, walking to the car park and seeing Harry Bannerman. I will never forget his words: 'You're on your way now.' I could tell by the way he said it that he was pleased for me, and that meant a great deal. That was really my arrival on the scene. I finished second in the Benson & Hedges later that year, but really the 1976 Open, suddenly coming from nowhere, that was when I felt I belonged.

The Benson & Hedges, where Australian Graham Marsh's last-hole eagle would prove crucial, was a rewarding exercise in many respects, not least in the shape of the runners-up cheque of £5,000, and I was indebted to my temperament which kept me calm in situations where I could have been forgiven for getting a little nervous or tense. The *Daily Telegraph* reported on my third-round 66: 'James is his own most severe critic and he refused to get excited about his round. Indeed, I doubt he would be much moved by a 59.' Pat Ward-Thomas took that comment a step further: 'The impressive feature of James' last round at Fulford was the way in which he preserved his rhythm. He drove steadily, pitched with a nice, contained swing and attacked the course from the outset, not playing defensively as many similarly placed would have done. He is a quiet, reserved young man who seemed strangely unimpressed or even elated about his success. This may stem from an enviable calm, and I suspect he is a perfectionist. That, too, is a virtue if it is not overdone.'

My demeanour has often been a cause for comment, although I still cannot understand why. I remember a couple of photographers posing me with my record-breaking card at Birkdale, one of them urging me to smile. 'It's no use,' I said, 'I can't.' I had always had difficulty in that department. People would come up to me and say 'Cheer up!' when I was just sitting there quite normally. I just looked sad. Finishing the season with a record £13,000 for a newcomer and winning the Rookie of the Year title attracted a certain amount of attention from the press. I was never particularly surprised by doing as well as I did, but always a little puzzled that people should make a fuss about it. One reporter described me as 'the perfect example of an anti-hero, a loner who remains a stranger to most of the other fellows on the Tour'.

As a 22-year-old, having played the game for a decade and never really having changed my approach, I always believed that I had a very good chance of making it. I always felt that if I hit the ball properly the results would follow, and it never worried me that people thought me a little odd, if by that they meant that I went my own way and had little time for socialising. I hated all the formalities and cocktail parties that were part of the Walker Cup and was quoted at the time as saying, 'I just sat down and went to sleep. They're a waste of time and energy. I guess they must please someone, though. I try to be friendly to people though I fail most of the time, but I make the attempt. I'm very tolerant of people. I am, it's true. But I don't go out of my way to smile on the golf course. I've never tried to present any image out there. It's difficult enough trying to get the flaming little ball into the hole without thinking about other things.'

It was true that I saw little of the other pros away from the course because I preferred small hotels and was quite happy to go back after playing to spend a quiet evening with a book and a plate of fish and chips. I did not drink then – alcohol, tea and coffee were not part of my diet – so there was little point hanging around the clubhouse. I liked to live life as I wanted and just preferred the simple things. I have never been the sort of person who gets really excited about anything, and I'm convinced we are born to be what we are. I have never been able to understand why some people want to make us what we are not.

Perhaps Dai Rees, the outstanding Welsh golfer, hit on one of the reasons why I made a successful transition to the paid ranks. He wrote in *Golf Monthly*: 'James has been successful in his first year as a professional because, unlike many other good amateurs who have turned professional and not immediately done well, he has not fallen into the trap of thinking that professional golf is an entirely different game. He has stuck with his amateur game and practised hard. And he has a fantastic temperament which defies anyone to know, by looking at him, whether he is scoring well, badly or indifferently.' And the late Richard Dodd, formerly golf correspondent of the *Yorkshire Post*, had this to say about my first season:

Mark James, variously described as untidy, sullen, dull, exciting, disinterested, intriguing and promising, is already something of a star after only a year as a professional.

He stepped from the amateur ranks into the professional game with none of the usual fears. He was not overawed by the thoughts of rubbing shoulders with the best golfers in the world because he has never had thoughts about other people's golf. He decided to play golf for money based on his own known ability. He was not prepared to change his swing, his dress or his personality to fit the accepted pattern and went about his business methodically and without fuss.

Despite his short apprenticeship, James has often said that professional golf is no different to amateur golf. He said last September after finishing second in the Benson & Hedges International Open at Fulford: 'I just play my normal game and I know I can start winning tournaments.' It seemed a presumptuous statement, but those who listened were quickly convinced that this young Lincolnshire lad was someone special. He is not given to boasting. He just has absolute faith in his own ability.

James cut a lonely figure during last season's tournaments and did not seem to make many friends among his new professional colleagues. He did not seek friendship because he wanted to beat every professional he met. But he collected many fans during his journey throughout Europe and Britain – not for an outgoing personality or exuberant nature, but for his single-minded approach to a task in hand.

James has been talked about more than any other young professional because of his unhappy appearance and slightly eccentric attire, and he apologises for his dour attitudes. 'I don't smile much because I'm not made that way,' he said. 'But I'm happy inside when I'm playing golf. I can't help it if my face won't smile.'

I have always found it easier to smile from inside (it makes a good excuse anyway), and there had been a few in an interesting, rewarding and occasionally strenuous first season that prompted me to take two months off in the winter to recharge. The rest paid off as I started the following year in Africa, and after finishing third in Nigeria moved on to Lusaka to claim my first big victory as a professional. I edged out Garry Cullen to claim their Open and, according to the *Evening Standard*, started smiling, though I'm sure they must have been exaggerating.

Columnist and television commentator Renton Laidlaw pointed out: 'James has what it takes to be a real winner. He has a solid game and hates to lose. Maybe James at times swears like a trooper when things go wrong on the course. Maybe he does bang his clubs in the ground and take divots unnecessarily when he hits a bad shot. Maybe he does look remarkably miserable and angry when he misses a putt, but he has fire in his belly and maturity will cure him of his bad habits.'

I was more interested in acquiring good habits in terms of my swing, technique and approach to the game, and I knew that if these were going to come about then it would only be through regular practice. I also had to work hard on concentration, which is essential for a tournament professional because he has to shut everything out. This was where yoga helped me, and I practised regularly after my long sessions on the range.

But practice was not making perfect as quickly as I would have liked, and that year, despite an invitation to play in the Ryder Cup, was something of a letdown – so much so that occasionally I felt like quitting the game, an over-reaction that was rather typical of me at the time.

7. FIRST AT LAST

The bonus for being selected to play in the 1977 Ryder Cup was exemption to three tournaments on the US Tour. I decided to take them even though I had ended the season fed up with my game and declaring to anybody who might have been interested that if things did not improve I would be seeking alternative employment. I had slipped from a first-year fifteenth to twenty-fifth in the Order of Merit and that did not represent progress in my book. It was closer to disgraceful.

My game, thanks to a change to a split-handed putting grip, did perk up a little before I headed across the Atlantic, although I went there with no great expectations and little interest in making it a permanent affair. Living there did not have a great appeal, particularly because of all the travel involved and a lack of fish and chip shops.

The first time I actually tried for my card in the US was in 1983. I was on an appalling course and my game was iffy enough without trying to play off average fairways and putt on dodgy greens. Not surprisingly, I failed. The second time, in 1985, I got through pre-qualifying on quite a good course and then went to the finals at Greenleaf and made the cut, but just missed out on my card. I needed to birdie one of the last two but hit it in the water somewhere, so I was pretty close, but not close enough. I started to play particularly badly after that and produced more of the same in 1987. By then, the European Tour was spreading much further and gaining a truly international flavour, so by the time I started to play well again in 1988 I certainly wasn't going to risk that form by going to America for three years.

I had seen other players go over there and the results were far from encouraging. When they played badly it was like putting a stop on their careers, and it became difficult to arrest the downward slide. Confidence is shattered and occasionally lost completely when a player does not make enough cuts because the whole flow of your game vanishes. I did not want to risk that happening to me, particularly when I was in my mid-thirties – a time when you don't know how long you have left, to be honest, as an active Tour player.

If I had ever decided to make the move to America it would have been in 1979, but I don't think I was good enough, even though I'd looked it in at least one tournament over there. I have never regretted it, not least because the European Tour is so much more of a friendly place.

It was only after my unsuccessful (no cuts made) visit to the States, when the European season again got under way in April 1978, that my game finally turned round towards respectability, although I would never be totally satisfied – a trait which has never left me. I was in contention in quite a few tournaments before walking, in early May, into another brush with officialdom in Sardinia. I had been fined the previous year for withdrawing from an event in Portugal when I wrenched a knee, and there had been a couple of other little incidents which the press pieced together to build up a 'bad-boy' tag.

I was injured again in Sardinia, but I didn't want to risk another fine so I continued with my round although reduced to using just one hand. It's a good job I stayed on at school to do mathematics because after taking an 8 on the way to a front nine of 41 my back nine read 3–4–5–7–10–10–10–9–12, which gave me a grand total of 111 – the highest score ever by a professional in a major European event. It could have been worse, too: at the last, somehow I managed to get up and down from a bunker using just a putter and one hand. Tournament director George O'Grady had a word afterwards and mentioned something about my having played the last five holes in one over 10s, but I think I told him I had not had much practice playing one-handed golf. I was only 24 and the inconsistency of officialdom did confuse me.

I had withdrawn in Portugal the previous year because I had found it impossible to find a caddie and could have aggravated my injury pulling a trolley around the hilly course. I was still unclear as to why I had been fined on that occasion, so when I damaged my wrist in Sardinia I decided not to risk the wrath of the Tour's magistrates and opted to continue with one hand rather than walk off. As usual, all I succeeded in doing was walking into trouble again – something of a trait during my early years on Tour.

I did find it hard to control my temper when I played badly, and after being spoken to during my first season I tried to cut down on swearing and banging clubs, but controversy and trouble did seem to find me for a time even though I never went looking for them. On top of the Portuguese affair I had also been fined for damaging a club. I could have contested that one because I didn't deliberately harm the offending weapon – it just struck a tree while I was trying to hurl it into a lake. I had also been fined for what was termed 'flippant behaviour' at a prizegiving ceremony in Zambia, when I shook the envelope that was supposed to contain my cheque and showed the crowd there was nothing in it. Officialdom had a serious sense of humour failure on that occasion. Added to all these 'sins' now was an official reprimand over the one-handed 111.

It was not the last time I would be in pain that season because injury would again find me at the Sun Alliance Match Play Championship at Dalmahoy in July, though it couldn't prevent me making the breakthrough by winning my first event on the European circuit. A painful foot meant I had to take a shoe off between shots and I lost a four-hole lead over Brian Huggett, but thankfully I limped to success in extra time. I had claimed some other prominent scalps too belonging to players of the calibre of Seve Ballesteros, Tony Jacklin, Sam Torrance, John Bland, Manuel Pinero and Eddie Polland, and when I got to the final Neil Coles – or Ol' King Coles as he was often headlined – was waiting for me on the first tee. It turned into one of the most interesting afternoons of my career.

First prize was £8,000, a fair amount then; the runner-up's £5,000 was not to be sniffed at either. Before we started, Coles just happened to collar me when nobody else was around and said, 'Do you want to play for all this money this afternoon?' I had absolutely no idea what he was talking about. He repeated, 'Do you want to play for all this money, or should we just split the first and second?' My immediate thought was that this was Neil Coles, a superstar golfer who had been playing top-calibre golf for what seemed about half a century, so why was he thinking about anything else other than winning? I just said, 'No, let's play for it.' It didn't make any difference to me; even if I lost I would get £5,000, and that was fine and dandy in my book. It seemed incredible to me that anyone could enter a round of golf with that attitude, but maybe I'm being cynical. I don't think our exchange had anything to do with the outcome, but I beat Coles, who didn't play that well, to pick up my first winner's cheque in a Tour event.

I was in trouble again a couple of weeks later, this time with some of my fellow players whom I criticised for behaving more like 'British Leyland car workers or dockers' than professionals during the strike that halted the Dutch Open. Just because the sponsors, who had put up a sizeable pot, had misunderstood a rule about inviting ineligible Americans, it was a case of 'All out, lads!' I couldn't believe it. The Euro Tour's players' division should not have behaved like a trade union.

Missing the event in Holland – I had no interest in it when they deemed all prize money unofficial – was a disruption to my season I could have done without, and I played badly for the remainder of the year, although I still ended it having broken into the top ten in the money list for the first time. My seventh place earned me just over £19,000, which is about what you get for finishing fiftieth in the Open these days.

But I did have that all-important first win behind me and I was confident heading into 1979 that if I played myself into similar situations, I would prosper. I had had a few near misses before my success and now I was confident that the hardest one to win was out of the way and that if I continued to progress others would follow.

8. A BURGER AT BAY HILL

The lure of the greenback and the chance of broadening our experience proved too tempting to resist at the start of the 1979 season so Ken Brown, Brian Barnes, Howard Clark and I headed west for Orlando, Fort Lauderdale and Miami on the back of our Ryder Cup exemptions. If we were to perfect our games then America in March was not the worst place in the world to be.

I remember turning up on a Sunday at Bay Hill for the first of those three events and there was no one else there. Each of us was handed a cloth bag containing brand-new practice balls, and for the honour of hitting them we were relieved of the sum of two dollars. In those days it was a fair bit of money, but compared to having a semi-blind caddie with a hangover trying to pick them up it was a luxury well worth the cash, and the practice turf was just perfect. When we walked on the range we all thought it the best turf we had ever seen. Ken would pull his wedge out and just start hacking great lumps out of the manicured Kentucky Blue, Bermuda or whatever kind of grass it was. It was sacrilege, and by the time the rest of the Tour got there, there wasn't much grass left. Put Ken on a range for two days and it looked as though it had been attacked by a JCB, although I must admit I was rather proficient in the art of earth-moving myself.

The practice facilities really were fantastic over there in those days, but of course a lot of the courses had purpose-built ranges while the vast majority in Europe didn't because they had been constructed so long ago. It would take another ten years really for facilities on the European Tour to improve noticeably. For those of us with the chance to go to the US, it was great for our game. We would fly out, play three tournaments and then join our Tour in April having hit a monstrous number of balls. We would also have putted on great greens, played good courses and continued our learning. The only downside was the number of McDonald's we force-fed ourselves. We used to go there for breakfast, lunch and dinner because they didn't have my preferred alternative. Unfortunately for my waistline, I was becoming rather fond of them.

There wasn't much in the kitty for more than a burger at Bay Hill that year because the only money any of us picked up at Arnold Palmer's event went into my pocket. I was the only one to make the cut, but I was never in contention and finished seventeen shots back, collecting £260 for my week's play. There was an improvement in the Inverary Classic at Fort Lauderdale, for Howard also survived to the weekend, as did Peter Oosterhuis, who by this time was operating full-time on the American circuit after dominating in Europe during the early 1970s. I was fifth after three rounds, attributing my solid scores to practice-putting on the carpet at home during the winter, but remaining unconvinced that my career would be best served on that side of the Atlantic. Unfortunately I was blown off course during the final round and slipped to twenty-eighth, some fourteen shots behind winner Larry Nelson, but at least I was learning quickly and I was better off by almost a thousand pounds.

I was seventeen shots adrift the following week at the Doral Open, but I had made the cut in all three events and returned home convinced that I had the game to compete in America. Whether I had the inclination was a totally different matter, one I didn't expect to address for a few years. For now, it was home, more practice and a few more scrapes on and off the course.

I'm not 100 per cent sure who christened me Jesse on Tour – probably Sam Torrance – but the idea may have come from an article highlighting my withdrawal from the first round of the Madrid Open in April 1979 because of hay fever. I had tied a handkerchief across my face to try to keep the pollen at bay and it was noted that my appearance was more that of Jesse James than professional golfer. I also missed the next event, and returned to Lyon the week after to discover my aptitude for finding trouble had not disappeared. Returning to my hotel room after a pro-am, I felt more like a proper Jessie when the lift jammed between the third and fourth floors. The only way out was to climb through the trap door in the roof, scale a ladder on the side of the shaft and escape at the next floor. The operation was successfully negotiated and I escaped unscathed, though I did need a bath.

Fate seemed to be conspiring against me, but fortune was beginning to smile, and never would that smile be broader than in mid-June at the Welsh Classic at Wenvoe near Cardiff. It would be my first stroke play victory in Europe and another significant milestone as I pipped Scotland's Mike Miller and Ireland's Eddie Polland at the third hole of a sudden-death play-off.

Typically, the tournament had not been without incident, for at the second hole of the final round I was the victim who wanted to perpetrate a crime. A spectator popped out from behind a tree as I played a recovery shot, the ball hit him and rebounded into the rough en route to a bogey. There was only one thing I wanted to do at the time and that was hit him with more than the ball, although for both our sakes I resisted the temptation.

Fortunately I survived, and just as important as the title and the £5,000 winner's cheque was the realisation that I was now on the threshold of the 1979 Ryder Cup team. Throughout my career I have never set goals above trying to do the best I can, because if you have targets and achieve them it can lead to complacency, and if you don't then frustration can develop and damage your game. But I did want another crack at the Yanks and they were now on the horizon.

But first it was my favourite event of the entire calendar: the Open. I like links courses, so I think that's why I have generally got a good record in the Open. I'm comfortable there and don't get too claustrophobic off the tee. If you do hit in the rough, you can usually get it somewhere up by the green and get up and down because the greens are high quality. The bunkers all have good sand, so that's another comfort, but over the years the R&A have really toughened up the championship courses, grown the rough very, very long and made the fairways very, very tight. That immediately makes me feel uncomfortable, notably in 1986 at Turnberry and in 1999 at Carnoustie. When they get that tight and the rough gets that long it tips the balance too much towards driving for my game, because I've never been that straight a driver. I have been a reasonable driver, but not good enough to cope with the type of course that was presented in 1986 and 1999. They were not quite as penal back in the 1970s, and I had finished fifth at Royal Birkdale in 1976, though never in contention. Two missed cuts later, I was back for the weekend at Lytham and aiming for just one thing: triumph.

The popular press seemed more concerned by my eating habits than my swing or championship chances and almost made it sound as if I were some kind of cannibal after I let it slip that I enjoyed steak raw. No matter how I ordered my cow it always seemed to come to me looking like a cinder, so I decided to order it just with its horns clipped and backside wiped. The headline writers had a field day, but I had other things on my mind during four days of the toughest competition I had ever faced.

The steaks were not the only raw things at Lytham because the weather was particularly fierce, but I ended the third day in joint fourth place alongside somebody called Jack Nicklaus, just one shot behind Seve Ballesteros and three adrift of American Hale Irwin. I believed I had a great chance of victory and knew one thing for certain: I would definitely be making a fight of it. I had never looked forward to a round with greater enthusiasm. Even the legendary Henry Cotton, a former three-time champion, told millions on television, 'I think this boy can do it.'

The Golden Bear was alongside me on the tee, but I felt neither in awe of him nor the occasion. It was a point the *Guardian* had made that morning, commenting on whether or not I was a champion in the making: 'Those who know him well believe it is difficult to put a limit on what he could achieve in this game if he put his mind to it. He has a genuine flair for golf, as opposed to a mechanical swing, and such players are unpredictable because the feel on which they rely to bring the club to the ball varies from day to day. If he has the essential feel in the final round he should give a good account of himself because he will certainly not be overawed by the enormity of the Open Championship.'

Too true, but for whatever reason, my start was nothing better than disgusting, particularly my putting. Even though I felt I was still in there with a chance after eight holes I was always playing catch-up, and Seve Ballesteros was in no mood to be caught. The occasion was mostly memorable for one particular shot that almost hit Big Jack on the leg. My second shot to the last finished left of the bunkers on the left-hand side of the green. Unfortunately the pin was tucked left too and I was left with an impossible pitch over the bunker. The Golden Bear thought he was standing well out of harm's way, but I shanked the shot straight towards him and he had to jump out of the way pretty quickly as the ball skittered across the green and stopped on the brink of a bunker on the other side. I holed it from about 40 feet for a par and finished fourth. Jack took it in his stride. He had seen me play for seventeen holes so I think he knew that anything could be expected.

Although I bettered overnight leader Irwin by five shots, my 73 left me in fourth place, a shot behind Nicklaus and Ben Crenshaw and four back from Seve. There was no reason to be downhearted, though, because the £7,500 I received put me third in the Ryder Cup standings.

So I would be going to America, but only for the Ryder Cup, because I had now revised my thinking on trying for my US Tour card. I just didn't consider that the time was right and had not been fooled by making all three cuts earlier in the year. What Seve was doing would boost the development of the European Tour, and although I felt I would have to try America at some stage, it would only be when I was good and ready. I didn't want to go until I was confident I could win at least £50,000 a year because I was not interested merely in making the top 60. The name of the game was making money, and unless I felt I could make a lot more there than I could in Europe, which was developing quickly in terms of prize money and numbers of tournaments, then I was staying put. Neither did I want to play more than 28 events a year, and if I went there I would be spending six months on each circuit and playing 35, and that would be too many. No, America could wait – not that I expected any great feelings of loss on their part.

I was definitely enjoying myself in Europe, whatever my on-course demeanour might have suggested, and a second win that year came at the Carroll's Irish Open at Portmarnock thanks to a record-equalling 65 in the last round. I went home with my hands on the trophy and my first five-figure cheque. By the end of the season my earnings totalled £32,494 and I had finished third in the Order of Merit, my highest position to this day and, I suspect, any other.

9. REAL CRACKER

My relationship with the press has often been strained to say the least, although in 1999 I did make a conscious effort to satisfy their every wish before, during and after the Brookline Ryder Cup. As captain I figured it was better to have them on board than sniping across our bows, and generally speaking I got a very fair ride with the boys and girls from the Fourth Estate.

That had not always been the case. I had a big problem with shorthand, particularly during my early years on Tour. I have no idea how it works, but it has always seemed to me that it goes down on the page one way and comes out another. I was being misquoted far too much, so I decided not to give interviews in shorthand any more because I preferred people to report exactly what I had said. It rarely happened, and it made it so difficult for me to have a relationship with them that I occasionally considered barring myself from the press tent. A lot of the stick I received in the newspapers was either embellished or unnecessary. Other players did things that were left unreported, but if I so much as lifted a finger it seemed to be headline news. If anything went wrong it seemed to be a case of 'Where's Jesse?'

The answer at the start of the 1980 season was America, using my Ryder Cup exemptions again rather than going to Zambia and Kenya where I invariably seemed to get into trouble. I had taken a long break over the winter and it proved too long because I missed the first two cuts in the US. I survived in Miami and was in contention at the halfway point, but unfortunately they play tournaments over four rounds and I trailed away at the weekend.

Ken Brown and I did make a conscious decision to try to avoid trouble, and it was while we were in Rome after returning from America that we struck a bet: whoever was the first to be disciplined and fined that season would give the other £500. My recollection of the outcome of the wager is sketchy, but there was only ever going to be one winner. I would have pocketed the cash for certain because Ken and trouble walked down every fairway together, and particularly slowly. Ken insists we struck the bet because we both felt we had reached our peak in the world of attitude. Like me, he cannot remember who won, but he would have been fined, for slow play if nothing else, and then have let me forget that he owed me. I would have done the same to him, because £500 was a lot of cash.

I enjoyed playing practice and tournament rounds with Ken, but not behind him because he frequently came to a complete standstill. His playing partner would hit his shot, then all of a sudden it would occur to Ken that he might have to put his glove on and do the same. By about 1980 he was starting to make a big attempt to play quicker, which was probably just as well since a year or two later he joined the US Tour full time and in the 1980s they came down a lot harder on dawdlers than in Europe. In the space of three or four years, Ken went from a very average striker to an absolute flusher and enjoyed considerable success in the States, culminating in his 1987 Southern Open victory. Ken eventually took his dedication, enthusiasm and talent for preparation into the world of commentary, and again has risen to the very top of his profession. That is not just the opinion of the public but also that of Tour players, who can be difficult to impress to say the least.

But Ken was not there when I made my first trip to the US Masters in April 1980, and it's a pity I didn't make more of it because it also turned out to be my last invitation. Not that I was barred by the Augusta National power barons or anything like that, I just never got the chance again. I missed the cut by the two shots I dropped in the last two holes of the second round.

At least there was always the Open to look forward to, although Muirfield is another of my least favourite venues. I have always found it a bit nondescript, and if there's little wind it's particularly easy unless they have tricked it up. Still, maybe it's just my view and the way I play it that makes me indifferent to it; everyone else seems to think it's a good course, and sometimes you have to bow to public opinion, or at least the opinion of your peers. Mind you, had I won an Open there my house would be called Muirfield, my car would be called Muirfield, I would be using Muirfield clubs and wearing a Muirfield sweater.

En route to Muirfield that summer I finished second to Greg Norman in Sweden, so I arrived in Scotland as confident as it was possible for me to be. The only names above mine after the first day were those of Tom Watson and Lee Trevino. I was moving in exalted company, but not for long as a second-round 72 took me out of the top ten. Unfortunately, the downward trend continued, and by the end I was 21 shots behind Watson.

The one thing I did discover on the links east of Edinburgh was very sobering, even for a teetotaller: my putting had deteriorated to worse than diabolical and something needed to be done. Three- and four-putts were becoming the norm rather than the exception, and I became so worried that I literally could not take the club back. Experiments led me to switch to a split-handed method that might not have been ideal but at least allowed me to continue without freezing over the ball. I had tried the method briefly a few years before and discarded it. This time it would last longer following a chance encounter with a couple of hustlers at the Irish Open. From behind the ropes they somehow decided I was ripe enough to pluck on the practice green and challenged me to a duel for £20. I didn't like the idea of taking money from them and warned them they were in trouble, but they insisted. I would not normally encourage hustlers, but these two guys were cocky with it and I decided their money would be better off in my pocket. I tried out the new method and they left shortly afterwards – wiser, but poorer. At least they gave me a confidence boost exactly when I needed it most, so to that extent I was in their debt. The dividends were immediate, because even though I continued to switch and change I managed to hold off Brian Barnes to successfully defend the title by one shot.

Not that my putting ever reached acceptable levels, and at the Bob Hope British Classic at the RAC Country Club at the end of September I decided to teach one offending weapon a lesson. I had missed nine consecutive putts of ten feet and under during my second round, and that was seven or eight too many. I took my putter into the car park and gave it a good kicking. I bent it, scratched it, scraped it on the ground and tried everything to break it. I then hurled it into a hawthorn bush where I left it overnight in the hope that somebody would find it and take it away. If

anybody did spot it they obviously had far too much sense
to bother with it and left it alone. The following day I
retrieved it, put a new grip on and promptly netted eight
birdies in ten holes. It was obviously not a stupid putter
and wanted no repetition of the previous day's hammering.

The most memorable thing about 1980, however, was
my marriage to Jane Finch, the gorgeous daughter of an
Otley butcher. Girls had pretty much passed me by during
my youth. I don't know if it was the way I looked or my
use of some horribly inadequate chat-up lines – 'Have you
ever hit a four-iron off a hanging lie?' and 'I can get up and
down out of a lady's handbag' are not the biggest bird
pullers in the world – but a serious relationship had not
appeared on my life's itinerary. Then, about the middle of
1976, just after the Open, I got a call from a chap called
John Greetham, who is sadly no longer with us. He was
involved with Otley Golf Club and wanted me to come up
and play in an exhibition match on 10 October. I agreed,
and when the time came I got in my car to go and make
an exhibition of myself for the princely sum of £150,
which actually then was a nice payday. I couldn't exactly
go out and buy a new house with it, but it was certainly
worth travelling north to the Arctic Circle for.

When I arrived at the gates of Otley Golf Club and told
them I was due to play in an exhibition, they weren't too
impressed, so I had to pay to get in. At least they gave me
a programme, which would have been a prized possession
had I kept it (like so many things when you're young, you
don't bother keeping them, then twenty years later wish
you had). I went in, met the appropriate people and,
funnily enough, on my way to the first tee I noticed a

lovely-looking girl bending over doing up her golf shoes. She was only there, apparently, because her parents had had a bit of a barney over a waiting Sunday lunch and had just gone to the club to get out of the house. It was love at first sight, at least for me. It may have taken Jane a little longer, but she eventually got there, thank goodness.

We met properly after the match. I was hanging around having a Coke in the bar and she said words to the effect of 'cheer up, it might never happen'. Obviously I put her straight and told her I was perfectly happy. We got chatting and I asked her if she wanted to go somewhere else for a drink, and it went on from there. We went to a pub close to Otley called the Chevin, on top of a hill of the same name. I thought she was a cracker – still do, actually. She was intelligent and had a great sense of humour. To say I was fairly smitten is to understate my feelings as they were then and as they are now.

We started going out, although it wasn't that easy. I was away a lot and she not only worked but lived a couple of hours from me, but we saw each other when we could. I got £150 out of the day and a wife. I don't know how much it's still costing me, but it was worth it. Jane has been incredibly supportive for a long time, though she has never been slow to give me a kick up the arse if I've been out of order on the course or need to get out and practise. Jane, without doubt, has been a very good thing for me, and I would like to think I have brought a little something into her life, although for the life of me I cannot think what it might be apart from a few vegetables.

Jane has rarely swung a club since we met, but she used to do some work for a charity called Birdies and Babes at golf tournaments in the 1980s, and they used to put on a husbands and wives match. Before one of them at Birkdale, we went on to the range beforehand so she could hit a few balls, and she knocked it away quite well. She was hitting three-woods and quite nicely too, so I said that perhaps she should try the driver. I teed a ball up for her and gave her the driver – a weapon I had only had for a few weeks and one that I was starting to become very fond of. It was her first and last shot with it because as the ball disappeared into the distance the head went hurtling after it.

It has not always been easy for Jane to keep her head either when watching me play at tournaments. She has always been quick to defend me outside the ropes, particularly against those dim spectators who criticise out loud when there's every chance there's a relative of the player in the gallery somewhere. She has been a huge support to me in so many different ways, and certainly during my illness. She was there every day after my operations, every day during the chemotherapy. Her support meant and means an awful lot, and to be honest I just don't know where I would be or what I would have done without her.

10. CADDIE CHAOS

The year 1981 would see me drop out of the European Tour's top ten for the first time in four seasons – a situation that would prevail until 1988. At least, as always, there was the Open at Royal St George's in Sandwich to look forward to, and after a fifth and fourth place previously I had every intention of going better. I did. My third place behind American Bill Rogers remains to this day my best finish in the world's oldest and best championship. If I was ever meant to win a grand slam event it would have been an Open, but fate decreed it was not to be.

My form had improved from abysmal (four cuts out of five missed, and it probably would have been a full house had there been a cut in the fifth event) to tolerable in the run-up to the Open. Two top-ten finishes in the preceding two weeks sent me heading towards the Kent coastline believing I was far better value than the 100–1 on offer at the bookie's. Sandwich is a tough test at the best of times, and this year would prove no exception. The course changes direction regularly, a real mix of holes, and although there are some blind shots – quite often the landing areas are flat – there is nothing worse than a blind shot into a sea of hillocks. The bunkers are reasonably fair and you can see most of them, in fact I think you can see pretty much all of them, but then there is a tough finish.

Nobody broke 70 during the first round and I was among those in ninth place after an opening 72. A second-round 70 improved my position to sixth, and at the end of the third round I was in second after posting a 68, the only bogey-free round of the day. But by this time Rogers was five shots ahead, and it became clear very quickly at the start of the final round that if anybody were going to catch the tall Texan, it would not be me. Rogers dominated throughout to win by four from Germany's Bernhard Langer, while I came in alongside the American Ray Floyd who, like me, would go close but never lift the silver claret jug. In his case, a victory in the Open would have meant completing a career grand slam.

At least my putting was only of semi-serious concern rather than terminal, and I had surprised myself by doing as well as I did. Royal St George's is definitely one of my favourite courses despite the blind shots and the fact that many of my peers seem to be fairly unimpressed with it. But regardless of the course, the Open is the Open and I've always enjoyed it. I like the pressure, the big stage, the crowds and the atmosphere. I thrive on it, actually, and I always try like hell whatever people might think about my appearance, gait and expressions. To be honest, I have never really been overly bothered by what they thought anyway, definitely not in those days, although I was beginning to mellow now that I had a wife to keep me in check.

Jane was with me in São Paulo in mid-October for the Open there, and it coincided with our first wedding anniversary. I decided to celebrate by winning the tournament, although not before I got severely upset again with my putter. This time it avoided serious punishment, but only just. It's difficult to imagine my winning a tournament and being totally jarred off with my putting. So maybe those who considered me *non compos mentis* did have a point.

To finish 1981 fifteenth in the money list was not my idea of improvement, and I was determined to rectify the situation the following season. Returning to Sardinia – scene of my infamous, one-handed 111 four years previously – brought proof that I had to some extent exorcised the gremlins from my game, although there were far too many of them to expect a complete cure. I had gone there having listened to coach Gavin Christie call me a foolhardy so-and-so for my course management skills, and I was under instructions to play safe for the first three months of the year to see how things developed. The order paid off, as did having caddie John Moorhouse on the bag – a real bonus at that time because he was recognised as one of the best readers of greens in the Caddie Fellowship, despite claiming on occasion that a wonky eye misled him. The 120 putts I had for the week was not only my lowest career total, but also a testimony to his skills. We usually agreed on lines, but if he said it was left to right and I thought the other way, I would just hit it straight. For most of the week in Sardinia I could not keep the ball out of the hole no matter how I tried, so much so that after eight holes of the final round I was eight shots clear. Unfortunately the lead did nothing for my concentration and I started to fritter away shots – thinking about winning rather than just hitting the ball. But I held on to win by three from American Bobby Clampett, he of the knicker-bockers at the Open and now an American television commentator.

The change in my attitude, due to marriage, and style, due to necessity, had not gone unnoticed among some members of the press. The late Peter Dobereiner wrote in *Golf World*:

He has always been the most intuitive of British golfers, playing by feel and instinct and paying scant heed to the niceties of style. That is not a criticism: we would all play better if we paid less attention to leg action or a ramrod left arm and allowed our instincts free rein.

However, in the case of James, I feel that his intuition came into conflict at times with the laws of dynamics. He stood wide open, 45 degrees away from the target line, and played the ball from an extremely forward position with a pronounced flailing action. When the inspiration was upon him, he played superbly, qualifying for the description of a natural genius, but the complexities of his method made his play inconsistent. For every deviation from orthodoxy he had to compensate, and it did not always work.

Now under the guidance of his coach, James is working towards a simpler, more orthodox method. It will take time for him to adjust, for a fundamental change of style involves much more than an adjustment of stance and ball position. He will have to work all the habituated eccentricities out of his system. With work and patience he will surely emerge as a better player, and if he can retain his inherent genius then he too could become a truly great player. He has proved that he has the stomach and the heart to endure the fiercest competition. With a technique to match his personal qualities he would be a formidable player indeed.

Just how formidable I was, I don't know, but I was certainly never shy of work and determined to make the most of my game.

Another £9,000 came my way in September at the

Hennessy Cognac Cup at Ferndown when a couple of 64s helped me to the individual prize and also team honours with Great Britain and Ireland over a Rest of the World side, much of my own success courtesy of a putting lesson from Ian Woosnam. Golf is unique in that players are never reluctant to help one another even though the tips they pass on may ultimately work against them. Woosie is no exception. He's always ready to spare a few minutes and he spotted a flaw in my technique and was more than happy to help out. It was much needed because my putting had got into such a state that my caddy had taken to carrying a crucifix in his wallet in the hope that it would keep the devil at bay when we were on the greens. Now that's what I call faith (if not in me).

John Moorhouse – although he was called Moorcash because he was always asking for more money and started wage negotiations for any year in the August of the previous one – was one of the best caddies I have ever worked with, and he took particular delight in my individual Hennessy Cup success over Nick Faldo because he had worked with him before leaving to join me. Our relationship was not without its lighter moments, the most memorable coming during a practice round with Mark Mouland in Italy one year when he was not exactly flushing it and I was nothing short of atrocious. The course had a collection of lakes, all with a base of what looked like plastic blue lino. I managed to find the water on the ninth twice and they were my last two balls. Moulie was also low on ammunition so I invited John to take off his shoes and socks, roll up his trousers and wade in for them, as well as any others he might find to see us through the round. He reluctantly agreed, paddled about picking up the balls, then suddenly started to slide on the lino towards deeper water. It was a fairly consistent slope and he just could not stop himself. First the water came over his knees, then it was up to his waist. Before long he was left with no alternative but to swim for it. He never did bring back any balls so our round ended there with Mark and I rolling around on the floor clutching our stomachs.

John was an excellent caddie, but he had an unnerving habit early on in our partnership of saying, just as I pulled a club out and went to address the ball, 'Watch out for the bunker on the right.' I got him out of that custom quite quickly, and we had a very good relationship until he decided to pack it in, settle down and get married.

One well-known bag man, George Leigh, had no idea what he was in for the one time he caddied for me. We were on the right-hand side of one hole very close to a really steep bank of brambles and nettles, peering up at the green and debating which club to take. We were trying to decide between a two-iron and a three-wood and eventually went with the wood. Now, I have a habit of flipping the clubs out of the bag pretty quickly, and unfortunately George hadn't quite got his head out of the way and got caught straight under the chin. He fell over and rolled all the way down the bank into the nettles, wondering what time of day it was. I was incapable of hitting a shot after that and George was never as keen to caddie for me again.

I teamed up with another caddie, who I assume is gainfully employed in another field these days, in Majorca. He was a lad from Liverpool and not very good, but the only one I could get at short notice. He said he knew a bit about football, but not much about golf. He was not a natural caddie, but things were going OK by the time we reached the turn and I handed him the putter and walked off to the tenth. Minutes later he'd still not turned up, so I told my playing partners to hit off and I would catch them up. Retracing my steps, I was halfway back to the ninth when I spotted him sitting inside a catering hut eating burger and chips with a large Coke. I wasn't at all happy and asked him what the hell he was playing at. 'I thought it was half-time,' he spluttered. He did not last long on Tour, and for the rest of the time he was there he answered to the nickname 'Half-time'.

Some caddies are real characters, and John 'Scotchy' Graham definitely falls into that category. I almost hypnotised him once. Thankfully we were not on the course, but at my house, in the early hours of the morning. We had had a barbecue after the Benson & Hedges one year and some of the players stayed over to watch the US PGA I'd taped while everybody was eating and drinking. It has to be said that Scotchy had had one or two, and he was lying on the carpet on his front, leaning on his elbows. At one point during the coverage I noticed his eyes were shut. I said to him, 'One seventy to the front, John, one eighty-two to the pin, five- or six-iron.' His head shook. 'There's a little bit of wind,' I continued, 'perhaps I'll go with the six.' His eyes were still closed, but he nodded and said, 'Yeah.' I said, 'Give me the six, then, John,' and he started to move his head round without opening his eyes. 'Where's the bag?' Maybe it was hypnosis, maybe it was the alcohol, who knows, but it was quite funny at the time.

John was, if not the first, one of the first caddies to go down full length on the greens to read the lines, and we were together for quite a few years. He was good fun, and it's always good to have a caddie with a bit of personality.

You spend a lot of time together and it can get a bit boring at times, but Scotchy was always good value.

I narrowly failed to get back into the top ten on the money list in 1982, but felt that 1983 would complete the journey. An early-season win in Tunisia proved encouraging although, surprise, surprise, it was not without its drama. I used the same three-iron I'd used all week to reach the last green and flew it comfortably by two clubs. This was where my gardening skills as much as my golfing skills became useful, because my ball ended in a bed of flowers and shrubs containing cineraria. They were similar to some I had back home in the garden, and I knew they were not to be tangled with, being of a particularly stringy variety. I somehow managed to flick the ball on to the green and two-putted for a two-shot win over American Tom Sieckmann and the two Gordon Brands.

I was on a roll, and had the chance to make it back-to-back triumphs in France a week later, but Seve Ballesteros had other ideas and I finally had to settle for third and a cheque for £2,235, although £50 of that had to be handed back in the form of a fine for forgetting to attend the prizegiving. I didn't attend the prizegiving at the Open that year either, but there was no fine. Having finished eighteen shots adrift of the victor I was not required to be there. It was not a particularly satisfying week, but although I finished way down, nothing happened to dull my enthusiasm for our only major championship.

Of greater concern that year was my being afflicted by a club-gripping equivalent of the stutter. It was nothing short of a mental block and very similar to the problem Spain's Sergio Garcia seems to suffer from occasionally. I just could not get comfortable with my grip, and at one tournament Ken Brown told me that on one occasion I waggled the club 35 times before I played a shot. It contributed towards my slipping to twentieth in the money list in 1983, and I was desperate to find a cure.

I was told of an American golfer who had suffered the same affliction. At address he had to count up twenty re-grips before hitting the shot. After months of club pumping he consulted a psychologist who suggested he address the ball and start counting the re-grips at eighteen. Incredibly, it effected an immediate cure.

I found my own remedy after a rest from the game: a slight change in grip, but more than anything else, willpower. But by this time I had lost my Ryder Cup place, although my form returned before the end of the season and twentieth place in the money list gave me exemption for the Open Championship.

11. HOME (NOT SWEET HOME) OF GOLF

If I was managing to keep out of trouble at this stage, my ball was doing anything but, and it cost me a successful defence of the Tunisian Open at the start of 1984. I was four shots clear of the field after six holes of the last round and playing nicely, but golf has a habit of kicking you where it hurts most, and this time it homed in straight on my wallet as the £10,000 winner's cheque ended up in Sam Torrance's pocket. My drive from the seventh tee bounced left into trees and finished suspended three feet off the ground on two small twigs protruding from the trunk of an olive tree. I jabbed the ball clear with the toe of my putter on to a sandy lie, from where I sliced a three-wood into the only bush on a step bank right of the green. I then hit a great left-handed shot out of the bush which trickled over the green into a four-inch-deep heel mark. I remember it as though it were yesterday: two to get out, two putts. My lead just vanished, and my head went with it on the way to a 78 and fourth place.

A runner-up spot to Brazil's Jaime Gonzalez in the Timeshare Tournament Players Championship at St Mellion in the second week of June put me in reasonable shape coming into the Open at St Andrews, but once again I was long gone before Seve Ballesteros sent shock waves of electricity through the auld grey toon with his air-punching salute following a last-hole birdie and victory over Tom Watson and Bernhard Langer.

I had paid my first visit to St Andrews in 1975, and it was far from love at first sight. Indeed, it was anything but.

I wasn't all that fond of the Old Course when I first played it then, and I have grown less enamoured with it since. There are a lot of blind or semi-blind shots and no consistent penalties for poor driving or bad iron play. I always get the feeling that if you hit a long way and putt well, you are pretty much bound to shoot a good score. I suppose you could use that argument for a lot of courses, but it seems to be exaggerated at St Andrews.

I'm told the course was meant to be played the other way around originally. I think on one day a year they still do that, and I think it might be a good idea to play that way all the time. Any change would be an improvement for me, but going back to front would put all the trouble on the left instead of the right. I'm not quite sure what effect that would have, apart from favouring the player who draws the ball rather than fades it because it's safer at St Andrews to set the ball off towards the middle of the course. But if you can carry the ball 270 or 280 yards off the tee it really doesn't matter which way you flight it, because you can fly a huge number of bunkers anyway.

Another of the problems with St Andrews is that it has never been upgraded to any great degree. I don't think they're allowed to add a single pot bunker anywhere without an Act of Parliament or at least a full meeting of the townspeople and a unanimous vote. Nothing has ever happened on the bunker front. Many of the traps are now outdated, and the ones that were just about in play in the 1970s are now 'carryable' for the long hitters. After Tiger Woods famously avoided bunkers in all four rounds when he won in 2000, one spread-betting company laid a quite ridiculous bet for the 2001 Open that it would be round about the back nine of the second round before he suffered that indignity. Anybody who knows the slightest thing about Lytham could tell you that it was a virtual certainty he would go in a bunker at least once in the first round. In fact, it only took him four holes, so that was probably the bet of the century for anyone in the know, and a few of my friends loaded in on that one.

At least at St Andrews they have lengthened a few holes by slapping in a few new tees, and that has helped to a small degree, but there are still a number of holes where the bunkers are at 270/280 yards and if you give it a lash you just go over them to a 100-yard-wide target. On holes like the fourth, in particular, if you hit a long way you can carry the humps and have a very big target area. Carry the bunkers on the right of the sixth and you have acres of room, and although there is a bunker slap-bang in the middle of the fairway on the ninth, it's no more than 280, I think, to carry it. The twelfth may not be as wide as some, but it's driveable; the bunkers on the thirteenth and fifteenth holes are usually out of play for the crushers; and the long hitters can reach the eighteenth unless the wind is against (it's normally helping). The joint first and eighteenth fairway is so wide you could land Concorde on it. It's crying out for a series of pot bunkers to toughen it up a bit.

Unfortunately, in modern-day golfing terms, St Andrews is pretty much obsolete. That doesn't mean I'd like to see it dug up, though. It's a wonderful place, and of course there's great history attached to it, but it's not really up to it in the twenty-first century. The only way they can actually make it at all difficult is to get the greens very, very hard and put the pins in places where you can't get to them. There are certainly enough slopes and hollows to allow that. My words might be considered sacrilege in some quarters, but although I do like the history of the game, it doesn't affect the way I play or the way I think or go about my business. I have a small collection of old golf books that are nice to look at occasionally, but I'm not a diehard collector or golfing history enthusiast.

After St Andrews, victory for me was not far down the line. It must have been a sweet one, too, because the press had a field day reporting the smile on my face as I came back from two down with two to play to grab a half against Manuel Calero and give England victory over Spain in the Hennessy Cognac Cup at Ferndown near Bournemouth. England captain Nick Faldo led the praise for my birdie–birdie finish by saying that it had taken a lot of bottle to achieve what I did. I don't remember hearing him say it because at the time I was submerged under caddies and team-mates on the last green.

Thirteenth on the Order of Merit did constitute a move in the right direction, but my six top-ten finishes in 1984 did not include a win, and I was rarely satisfied with my game or scoring. My putting, as ever, was in the lap of the golfing gods. Like me, they tended not to smile a great deal. The Ryder Cup was, as always, a definite target in 1985, but if my ambition was to be realised I would have to start winning again, and I had not taken a first prize for more than two years. I managed to put that right in Le Touquet in mid-May 1985 by claiming the GSI Open, but it was another occasion when things were not straightforward. Mind you, it would not have been me had they been.

I was sitting comfortably on a four-shot lead with just five to play when I hit my ball into the middle of a small shrub and was given a free drop from a rabbit scrape by official Alan Hibbert. My playing partner, Ronan Rafferty, disagreed and asked for a second opinion. Referee Andy McFee then declared my ball unplayable and therefore ineligible for a free drop. I had no hard feelings whatsoever with Ronan because everybody is entitled to an opinion, and in any event I scrambled a par after taking a penalty drop and held on for my ninth win. You may think that taking a penalty drop justified Ronan's objection, but had I been in tenth position I would definitely have played it. I nearly had a go at it to prove that it was indeed playable, but common sense prevailed.

Memories of earlier good times went with me to Sandwich for the 1985 Open, but a second-round 78 put paid to whatever hopes I had, even though I went twelve shots fewer the following day. I somehow managed to scramble back into contention and went into the final round believing I had half a chance. I was actually doing quite nicely, but my playing partner, the legendary Kiwi left-hander Bob Charles, had a really bad back and was struggling to tee it up, let alone hit it. We had lost probably three or four holes on the group in front, and after twelve holes he decided he couldn't take any more and walked in. I was left on my own, and it seemed to put me off. It's a poor excuse, I know, and I was definitely old and mature enough to cope with it at the time, but I immediately produced an horrendous finish. I dropped about six shots in the last seven. Had I played them in par or one under, I would have been very close to tying Sandy Lyle for the championship.

I was disenchanted when I left Kent, and it was a feeling that was to endure for the rest of a season during which my mind increasingly veered towards America. I was becoming ever more intolerant of our practice facilities in Europe and felt that my chances of improvement were being restricted. Put simply, I had had enough of the weather, the greens, the fairways and the ranges. This mood was in no way helped when I missed an eighteen-inch putt on the third extra hole of a play-off with Zimbabwe's Nick Price for the Lancôme Trophy at the beginning of October, and I was just as unhappy about missing out on the Ryder Cup again.

In November I went for my card in America but narrowly missed out. It was my last attempt. I played so badly the next two years it wasn't worth it, and then so well in 1988 I didn't want to rock the boat.

After missing four straight cuts at the start of 1986, my form was still of the stuttering variety when I arrived at Turnberry for the Open. The west coast of Scotland links is a classic course. As you play you get the feeling of winding through the dunes and meandering along the sea front. It is simply a series of good holes, and I think it may well be the best, certainly one of the best, on the Open roster. There is hardly a weak link on the course, and when the wind starts to blow towards you, you can go for plenty. Like all the classic courses it has a great finishing stretch, with the par-five seventeenth a real feature because you can make eagle there . . . and just as easily bogey. The eighteenth is another that gives you options and allows you to bite off as much as you can chew, depending on how your nerves are.

A first-round 75 for me was far from inspiring, but because of the tough conditions it was good enough for a place inside the top 25. I improved by two shots in the second round, but dropped down the order. A 73 was the lowest I could manage all week, and I finished sixteen shots behind Greg Norman.

Consequently, the first-round 65 I shot in the Benson & Hedges International at Fulford in mid-August came as a surprise, but it wasn't as startling as the attack by flying ants that halted play for twenty minutes while I stood with playing partners Hugh Baiocchi and John O'Leary, who were jumping about and yelling out in pain. The ants, for some reason, knew better than to tangle with me, but it was like watching a scene from a horror movie.

That was the last I saw of the ants, but not Baiocchi. He was at my shoulder when three of us set off towards extra holes, my missed three-foot putt at the last gifting the South African and American Lee Trevino another chance. It was something of an unplanned birthday present for Baiocchi, who was celebrating his fortieth at the time, but I was lucky enough to snatch it back on the first extra hole – not that I was all that confident having lost my previous two play-offs. Few, if any, of my 23 professional wins gave me greater satisfaction because this was my first success on English soil in my adopted Yorkshire, no more than twenty miles from home. I quickly forgave myself for an uncharacteristic show of emotion after winning. I launched my baseball cap into the late-afternoon air and my face broke out in a cabaret of smiles as the fifteen-foot birdie putt dropped into the hole.

Although I was not altogether dissatisfied with my lot come the end of 1986, it still nagged at me that I should finish better than about twentieth in the Order of Merit each season. I felt there was a top-five player waiting to get out, and I wanted to make the transition. In my eleven years on Tour so far I had only once been outside the top twenty, but only once inside the top five. I pledged to do something about it and continued all the hard work on mind, body and technique.

Concentration for me was a key aspect. I would often set myself targets of staring at something, anything, for ten minutes without having any intrusive thoughts, or I would set myself some complicated mental arithmetic and keep at it until I had worked it out. Concentration was one of the reasons I had what I prefer to call an 'expressionless' face while playing. I always felt that if anybody had to make an effort to look happy then they were not focusing on the task ahead. I was never, of course, a natural smiler, and I knew that if I tried to change now it would be to the detriment of my game.

I had been lucky in never having suffered particularly from nerves, my worst cases nothing more than a tingle on the first tee of the Open. I had never been one to feel under more pressure in a Ryder Cup than when trying to make the cut in a normal tournament. I had always given everything whether I was playing for a first prize of £10,000 or for a few bob with friends at home. So I was convinced that it was neither my concentration nor my nerve that was preventing me from moving to the next level.

Actually, I knew what the problem was. Unfortunately, I would never consistently find the key to being a good putter. Were I ever to look at a list of the top 150 putters, then to find my name I would work my way up from the bottom, and I wouldn't have to go very far. I was sure that if my putting had been only half as good as the rest of my game I would have won twice as much. I knew there were people who could pick up a club and immediately smash the ball miles, while others couldn't hit it out of their shadows no matter how hard they tried. Not being naturally good at putting was just something I had to live with. I had to be content with being competent and occasionally quite good through sheer hard work. I was a streaky putter and putted poorly rather too often, although, looking back, I was almost certainly better than I thought I was and probably quite reasonable.

I was prepared for plenty of tough graft heading towards 1987, another Ryder Cup year, but, surprise, surprise, fate was ready to ambush me.

12. PEAKS AND TROUGHS

I took a new putter and grip with me into the 1987 season, abandoning my split-handed method after seven years, and there were early indications that the move was a positive one. On 22 March, after three rounds of the Moroccan Open at Royal Dar es Salaam, I was just one shot behind Howard Clark. Unfortunately, I was still adrift after four, but I came out of Africa believing a new dawn was breaking over my career. It was – a false one. The frustrating irony was that my improvement on the greens coincided with a deterioration in my game off them. Such is the game of golf – or mine anyway.

For the first time in nine years I missed the cut at the Open, and without a big payday at Muirfield my chances of making the Ryder Cup team were slim. The year was summed up for me on 12 September, the first round of the Vernons Open at Hoylake, where an 84 constituted one of my worst ever professional rounds. My effort – for want of a better word, although I tried on every shot – included a nine, an eight and a four-putt. It seemed to epitomise a season I could not wait to get behind me. It was my worst round in my worst year – I was thirty-second on the money list – but it would be ten long years before I sank that low again, to some extent thanks to a Christmas present from my dad.

He dug out some old ciné films taken in the late 1970s and put them on, even though working that projector required a Masters degree in physics. Apart from the entertainment of seeing myself in action with a full head of hair – cut in a style described in less than complimentary terms by David Feherty as a cottage loaf – there were lessons to be learnt. I studied the film in depth, watched others competing in the major championships, and came to the conclusion that my problems centred on the fact that I had lost my late hit. I had been concentrating so much on getting my backswing correct that I had forgotten what I was doing at the all-important impact zone.

I had also asked Gavin Christie to conduct his own independent analysis, and we both came up with the same diagnosis and cure. It meant radical changes to my swing because of the discovery that I had been moving my hips laterally when I should have been turning them. A similar thing had happened with my shoulders, so we set about making the corrections. The subsequent improvement came as a surprise, and was extremely welcome.

From practice range to getting things right on the course went reasonably swiftly. It needed to, because I had an aim. Whenever I was mentioned in the press my name was often attached to the phrase 'former Ryder Cup player', and that was a situation I wanted to rectify over the next two seasons before the biennial tussle against America returned in September 1989 to the Belfry, scene of Europe's greatest triumph in 1985.

My preparation for the 1988 European season could hardly have gone better. Not only did I win the South African TPC, my longest second putt all week was no more than six inches – and even I don't miss from that range, although there had been times when I convinced myself that I could.

The omens were still good come the middle of May when the Tour reached Santander in northern Spain for the Spanish Open at Royal Padrena. It would be an event not without incident, although, thankfully, the only one involving me came when I was presented with the trophy at the end of four long days around Seve Ballesteros's home course. Seve was not a happy Spaniard – not because I won or shot my lowest ever round, 63, on his beloved track, but because of the way the European Tour officials had set up the course.

Seve complained bitterly that one of the great courses in Europe (although that was highly debatable) had been destroyed. It was an amazing attack. He claimed his recommendations had not been followed, though I was at a loss to remember when any player, no matter what his name or ability, had ever been given the right to set up courses the way he wanted. 'I would have hoped for more respect from the Tour than I have had this week,' he chuntered. 'I am very angry. The course has been set up for the British. Any championship at Padrena ought to be won with a score of around six under par, but the character has been changed so much this week that golfers who don't normally break par are shooting rounds of 63. I feel as if I'm playing the course for the first time this week.' His comments were born of a belief that the Tour had allowed the fairways to be speeded up (he wanted them slower) and the greens to be softened (he wanted them firm and fast). 'People who don't know will think that Royal Padrena is just a pitch and putt course. Maybe when I am not here they will appreciate they have lost something good for the European Tour.'

The case for the defence was presented by tournament director Mike Stewart, who said he had not been able to follow the advice on the greens because the grass would have died while they watered the fairways. Generally, they had made the best of what they had been given.

There were no complaints coming from my direction during the tournament, though afterwards I was a little more vocal and said that Seve was on a different wavelength to everybody else. 'He says one thing and the other 149 say another. Maybe it's because he's not used to losing.' I, on the other hand, hadn't been used to winning for a couple of years, but despite being chased home by the formidable figure of Nick Faldo, I managed to hang on.

I was interested to read television commentator and professional Alex Hay's assessment of me at that stage of my career in *Golf Illustrated*, because he came fairly close to getting to the nub of my swing and psyche.

I have watched Mark James's career with interest over the years and observed his marvellous highs and deep troughs of depression. I don't think there is another British golfer who gives spectators so much fun when he is storming to a par-shattering round, which he does regularly, yet who is capable of infuriating those same fans when he slumps into what appears a total state of indifference when things are going wrong.

The unfortunate thing about the low is that while Mark's criticisms are only directed at himself and rarely ever at others, his expressions and actions have an effect on spectators who get frustrated at seeing a golfer with such outstanding talent appear so miserable. He often fools the TV commentator, who, on seeing him slam his club into the ground after hitting a shot, claims, 'He's completely mishit that one!' only to see the ball pitch a few feet from the flag.

Above Aged 19 and already smiling for the press! (author's private collection)

Below Being presented with a memento of my win in the English Amateur Championship by the Marquis of Exeter (author's private collection)

Above Europe's 1979
Ryder Cup team at
The Greenbrier in
West Virginia (© The
Phil Sheldon Golf
Picture Library)

Right Ken Brown
and I lost 3&2 to
Fuzzy Zoeller and
Lee Trevino in the
morning fourballs on
day 1 at The
Greenbrier (© The
Phil Sheldon Golf
Picture Library)

Left Ryder Cup,
1977, Royal Lytham
and St Annes (© The
Phil Sheldon Golf
Picture Library)

Ecstatic at making the winning putt in the play-off at the 1986 Benson & Hedges International Open (© The Phil Sheldon Golf Picture Library)

Holding the B&H trophy aloft (© The Phil Sheldon Golf Picture Library)

Above Cutting the
lawn at our first
house
(© The Phil Sheldon
Golf Picture Library)

Right Celebrating
victory in the 1990
English Open
(© The Phil Sheldon
Golf Picture Library)

Left With Jane, thoroughly enjoying Europe's triumph in the 1995 Ryder Cup at Oak Hill
(© The Phil Sheldon Golf Picture Library)

Right In the thick of the action alongside Colin Montgomerie and Paul Lawrie
(© The Phil Sheldon Golf Picture Library)

Below Brookline, 1999. On the course with Sam Torrance and Derrick Cooper
(© The Phil Sheldon Golf Picture Library)

With Grace, Felicity and Edward, between chemo sessions. No hair, nice hat! (author's private collection)

Above Jane, Liz, Waddy and Grace, out on the town at Tony Dalli's restaurant near Marbella, August 2000 (author's private collection)

Left Back on the piste at last! With (from left to right) Will, Harvey and Tom Linden, Vail, April 2001 (author's private collection)

Below With Jane, at home (© The Phil Sheldon Golf Picture Library)

Mark's great problem in golf is that he is such a perfectionist that he demands a standard of performance that is difficult to attain, particularly as he plays with such an individual technique. His swing was designed in collaboration with his coach Gavin Christie, and I use the word 'designed' deliberately for many individual beliefs and practices were used that strayed from what would be described as the true orthodox method. I hasten to add that this does not mean they were wrong, but it does mean that when things go wrong it is necessary for the player and coach to get together quickly. Any intrusion by another teacher might damage the mechanism. Teaching also requires a sense of communication built over a long period and which understands temperament as well as physical ability.

In Mark's case, I have always observed that there is a great reach for width of arc in the backswing with the arms and shaft stretching away from the ball and the wrist movement fairly minimal so the shaft appears laid-off at the top. Then, as the downswing starts, the hands and wrists work in search of the most powerful place to attack the ball from, which in this process of swinging would give the appearance of a downward and inward loop. In other words, the wrists both prepare and act in the same part of the swing, the downward movement. The result is that Mark not only hits the ball from in to out, he hits it with incredible acceleration. His clubhead probably moves faster through the ball than any other player on the Tour.

We all know that clubhead speed, provided it is part of a wide arc, will generate great yardages, so Mark is recognised as a long hitter. We also know that generating such speed demands an incredibly fine sense of timing because the clubface is only square to the target for a fraction of a second. I realise that Mark has the ability to strike fast yet still keep the left hand ahead of the clubhead when it meets the ball, and few can do that. Nevertheless, to have such a movement and add it to the mentality of a perfectionist is a difficult combination. That is why when Mark slumps into one of his lows he feels much worse about the situation than the spectators feel he should.

Astute man, that Hay, but then all I was interested in was making it while the sun shone.

Unfortunately, I finished in it rather than made it at the Open when Seve Ballesteros forgot all his early-season complaints to win magnificently at Royal Lytham & St Annes, to date the last of his five majors. At least I was back to playing all four rounds, although a weekend of 74–76 meant I was closer to the foot of the field than the head.

But my career was back on track, and as I headed into yet another Ryder Cup year I felt confident not only in my game after finishing eighth in the money list, but also in my ability to make the Europe team. It had been over seven years since that had last happened, and that was too long.

13. GREEN FINGERS

I have always enjoyed playing golf in South Africa, and 1989 would be no exception, even though I failed to match the previous year when I won a tournament. I saw enough, however, to be as optimistic as I possibly could be – never too much – about a domestic season that would determine whether I was good enough to represent Europe at the Belfry, a venue that had developed into one of Britain's finest.

But it was several thousand miles away in the desert heat of Dubai at the beginning of March that I really knew my time had come again – and not before time, either, in my book. The Karl Litten Desert Classic was a newcomer to the circuit, but an extremely welcome one for a variety of reasons. It could go in the calendar at a very early stage of the season because, if it could guarantee anything, it was good weather. It also offered one of the richest purses on Tour and, as a result, high Ryder Cup points. Both would be very welcome because I had never hidden the fact that my biggest career aim had always been to make as much money as I possibly could.

The Ryder Cup had become very high-profile since Tony Jacklin had taken over the captaincy in 1983 and the likes of Seve Ballesteros, Nick Faldo, Sandy Lyle, Bernhard Langer and Ian Woosnam had established themselves as world forces, so it was never far from anybody's mind, most of all the press's. They quizzed Jacklin about me and the Cup. He generously thought I would be 'a terrific asset to the side', and also said that while he was categorically against appearance money in the biennial match, if the players were to be paid then it should not be less than £100,000 a man. 'You cannot recommend a penny less in view of the excruciating pressure these guys face,' remarked Jacklin, who also felt that the selection procedure, if it went to play-for-pay, would have to be changed to the top twelve in the money list and no wild cards. 'No one should have the right to say who earns that kind of cash,' he added.

The tournament in Dubai could not have been tighter: 72 holes could not separate me from Australian Peter O'Malley, our aggregates of 277 giving us a three-shot lead over England's Paul Broadhurst. I was fortunate to claim the title and the giant silver coffee-pot trophy at the first extra hole, and then I was asked if I would like to be a superstar. I have never been anything other than honest with my answers to the press and I told them that I could cope with success because it was a lot easier than coping with failure. Whenever guys talked about how tough it was to handle the pressure at the top, it always seemed to me that they had forgotten what it was like at the other end of the scale. It was not in me to complain about being successful. I knew it wouldn't be easy, but I saw no reason why I shouldn't become one of the world's best players, as long as I could get my putting to a more consistent level. I did recognise, however, that that was easier said than done.

I also understood the necessity to stick to a planned schedule no matter how far a good run of form could go towards changing it. But I had decided to take three of the next four weeks off, not least because of the need to plant beans, of the broad and runner variety, and sweet peas in my garden. I also understood the importance of relaxing. I knew what it was like to be over-golfed.

I have always found gardening comforting, even though it's hard work. It is a total change to everything else, and although it can never take my mind completely off other things, I have always been able to mull over problems better when messing about in my ground under repair at home. I find it therapeutic. The thing about gardens is that there's always something to do, even if it's just mowing, hoeing or a spot of watering. I even tried to make a green once, but it wasn't a great success (a bit like my putting) because I was never around often enough to look after it properly.

Although I enjoy having a few flowers and I particularly enjoy growing sweet peas, vegetables are my serious passion. They are so much tastier than the ones you get in the shops. The difference in something like broad beans is immeasurable. I never really liked them until I grew some for Jane but now they are among my favourites. When they come out of a packet they can be tasteless. But if I have a favourite, it would have to be mangetout.

Not that tending my garden ever took me away from the game completely; there was always work to do with my swing. It needed pretty much constant tinkering with, even though I had always disagreed with those who considered that what I had was not out of the textbook. It certainly was in the most important area – that of repeatedly getting the clubhead back square to the ball. Who was to say what was textbook anyway? Everybody has his own little quirk, but through the ball all the great players are very much the same. This was what I practised: the ability to get into this position effortlessly time after time.

It was certainly in the correct position when I completed a March double by winning the AGF Open at La Grande Motte near Montpellier to go top of the Order of Merit and ever closer to a Ryder Cup comeback. I had gone into my 1988/89 winter sabbatical with a damaged wrist but a positive attitude, thanks to the knowledge that technically I was swinging as well as I ever had. I'd come out for the new season in similar vein, and although the wrist was still bandaged it was quickly improving. Two tournament wins proved that.

The swing was key for me because I have never been a great believer, if at all, in golf psychology, which had been creeping into the game in ever more complex forms during the 1980s. I always felt that young players would be better advised to spend their time practising and learning their trade, for I saw mental analysis as a great way to make excuses for a bad swing. I felt a professional needed an open mind to both positive and negative aspects of his game; using crutches such as positive thinking and self-belief could have a harmful, long-term effect. All the top players had two hallmarks: common sense and concentration. I didn't believe the mental side of things extended beyond that, and little has happened since to sway me from those thoughts. Golf, for me, has always been 95 per cent physical and 5 per cent mental, although the fact that I have never had too many mental problems probably makes me see it that way.

There were few, if any, mental aspects to my golf during 1989 because I continued to play some of the best of my career. My third win of the season, in June at the NM English Open, could not have come at a more fitting venue, because success at the Belfry meant I would be returning there in September. No more 'former Ryder Cup player, Mark James' for me. The winner's cheque was significant – £41,660 was a tidy sum – but being back on the Ryder Cup team was equally important. I had been lying in joint sixth place going into the last round, but a timely 68 took me into a lead that only Eamonn Darcy had a chance to equal. The Irishman needed to birdie the last two holes, got one at the seventeenth and may have fancied his chances having almost eagled the last the previous day. I was in the press tent with Jane and her parents when Eamonn stood over a 30-foot birdie putt at the last. I rarely show emotion win, lose or draw, but I did breathe a sigh of relief when the ball stopped half a roll short of the hole.

My schedule did not include playing in the following week's Carroll's Irish Open, although I was a former double champion. My reasons for missing the event did not go down well with the press. I said that I had not fancied playing because the players' car park was a long way from the clubhouse, the practice ground was no good, the weather was grotty, everything was so expensive, there were kids running all over the place and the previous year the courtesy car people had refused to take my wife into town – not on a special trip, simply on their way to bring a player to the course. It was open season on Mark James again, and the press had a field day.

On the whole, my observations were light-hearted, although I realised later that I could hardly have expected those connected with the tournament to see them in the same light. I did regret saying what I did, but my comments were not meant in the way they were taken. Talking about the weather was a joke because I knew it wasn't always bad, and although my criticisms of the players' car park and the practice ground were serious, I really don't think they should have created such a fuss. Indeed, I was hoping the organisers might see it as constructive criticism and act on it accordingly. Unfortunately my words were not taken like that, and the Irish press particularly went out of their way to build something out of not a lot.

It was not the only time I fell out with the press in 1989. I was also slated in early July for allegedly storming out of Monte Carlo after qualifying for the last two rounds. Storming out? Nothing could have been further from the truth: I walked away quite calmly after making my decision. I knew the course wasn't doing my game any good, I didn't like Monaco and I wanted to go home, and that's what I decided to do. I broke no rules and actually received last-place money, but that didn't stop the press having their say.

I was fed up of being dumped on by the tabloids, so after that I decided that answers to any questions would be either yes or no. While many players and a few journalists were highly amused by my tactics, some of the members of the Fourth Estate were distinctly unimpressed. I felt justified in taking such action because I was thoroughly disenchanted with my treatment at the hands of the tabloids and even the odd holier-than-thou broadsheet. There was talk of a fine, but it was no longer the 1970s, and besides, I wasn't strictly speaking transgressing the Tour's regulations, just pushing the boundaries of our code of conduct to the limit. These days a player could probably get away with even more, particularly after the 2001 Dunhill Links Championship, when some outrageously negative and unnecessary reporting on several aspects of the event culminated in the tournament almost being pulled out of the 2002 schedule. The players and staff of the Tour were livid, and rightly so, because losing such an event would have been an enormous blow, especially at a time when the world's major economies were somewhat under pressure following the events of 11 September.

I refused to let any controversy cloud happy days spent on the course. Having coach Gavin Christie on Tour was no doubt one of the reasons why my good form continued throughout 1989. My fifth-place finish on the money list was my second best ever, and I would never better it again in my career. My putting had been consistently good (no misprint) all year. I was working with putting guru and inventor Harold Swash and progress had definitely been made. It had been a vintage year, and I was determined that there would be many more, which is why at the start of 1990 I returned to South Africa, often the perfect place for me to build up towards a European season. However, not having hit a ball for five weeks, the rust was clinging to my clubs. Furthermore, going there put me on the SANROC blacklist, and I was banned from playing in Sweden courtesy of their ever-hypocritical government. They never did appreciate the efforts of the sporting authorities in South Africa to achieve an integrated sports structure and constantly pursued a lemming-like 'put pressure on whoever's at hand' approach to the evils of apartheid. It certainly was not because of their stance that apartheid was eventually dismantled.

One benefit of finishing fifth in the Order of Merit the previous season was my first ever invitation to the US

Open, at Medinah, Illinois. It was a rare opportunity – indeed only my second, and the first had been a decade earlier – to play in a major outside Britain.

The swing changes of 1987 had had more to do with my bank balance than any statement of intent so far as the majors were concerned, but having had two decent financial years I had intended to gear 1990 towards the grand slam events. By picking and choosing where and when to play, I would only be operating on the best courses, not those which might harm my game. It would also give me extra time to practise the specific shots I would need on the championship courses. Part of my build-up included a trip to Muirfield Village for Jack Nicklaus's tournament, but it was much closer to home where I found my touch before heading across the Atlantic.

I have always enjoyed the subtleties of Woburn, and the Dunhill British Masters there on the cusp of May and June allowed me the opportunity to exploit them as well as push my career professional earnings over the £1 million mark. The thirteenth triumph of my career put me in good heart for the US Open. I had waited fifteen years for my first crack at this major, and although I felt it should have come earlier, it was probably only at about that stage of my career that I felt I had a decent opportunity of doing reasonably well. Armed with a £5 yardage book I went into battle at Medinah, but my first visit to the season's second major would not end in glory, but after two rounds instead – I missed the cut and waited another six years for the chance to do exactly the same.

I hoped for better things in the Open at St Andrews, and it certainly was hope more than expectation because I have often been a golfing pauper in the Kingdom of Fife. As I've said, I don't like the course and have never considered it a good test of golf. My game isn't suited to it either, because St Andrews is largely a putting contest. Any kind of poor shot will more than likely make the green, but in order to score well your putter has to be hot, and that's not my kind of golf. Tongue in cheek, I had often said that the biggest mistake I make at St Andrews is turning up, but that was because I had always found it a boring and straightforward course. Playing well, I would shoot 69; a bad round would result in a 73. I rarely shot outside those numbers, so I wasn't the least bit surprised with my first two rounds: 73 and 69. That meant I would be having another two rounds over the weekend, but not in contention because I was already ten shots adrift. I was fourteen back by the time Nick Faldo collected the trophy and not too unhappy about being on the road back to Yorkshire.

The US PGA had also invited me to their major at Shoal Creek in Birmingham, Alabama, but there I was to fare the same as at the US Open. I would need another couple of years before making a cut in an American major, the 1992 PGA at Bellerive, though I finished many strokes and a time zone behind Nick Price.

My season was all about Europe now and hanging on to my top-ten place, which I managed to do, but without margin for error. America might not have been a happy hunting ground, but the green, green grass of home proved far more lucrative as I managed to hang on to my English Open crown at the Belfry by defeating Sam Torrance at the first extra hole – thanks, to a certain extent, to my good friend and rival.

Sam was at the centre of everything that week because during the third round he hit the headlines when an eagle two at the tenth was turned into a birdie because of a rules infringement. A marshal noticed that he had waited longer than the permitted ten seconds for his ball to drop after he reached the hole, so his two became a three when referee Andy McFee watched it on television. At least it was sorted out before Sam signed his card, so there was no disqualification, but he entered the last round two rather than one behind, and that shot was enough to prevent him winning in normal time.

Indeed, it was Sam who put me on the straight and narrow during the last round when it looked as though my chances were disappearing after I unintentionally surrendered the lead. As we walked off the twelfth tee, Sam came over and said, 'What the hell's wrong with you? You're one shot out of second place, isn't that good enough for you? Get your finger out, we can still finish first and second.' I listened, did exactly what he said and promptly beat him in a play-off. There's gratitude for you.

Pro-am form is rarely an indication of what's going to happen once the tournament proper starts, but I was not going to hand back the 62 that went against my name in the curtain-raiser to the Lexington South African PGA Championship at the start of the 1991 season. Four sub-70 rounds during that tournament were not to be sniffed at, and good enough to get me into a play-off that ended for me with a sliced drive on the first extra hole. I notched up another second place in the South African Open, so I headed for Europe in good heart.

It might not have been too bad had I headed for southern Europe, but St Mellion, of the Cornish variety, was just a little too far north in April. There was more risk of hypothermia than any decent scoring in the Benson & Hedges International there, and I played four rounds in 35 over par – something of a result considering that I couldn't feel my hands and rarely my feet during the week. Actually, I was rather pleased with myself to return an 88 in the third round because it would have been very easy to fall to pieces. I was tempted at one stage to try hand warmers, but quickly dismissed that notion on recalling what happened the last time I tried them: I set myself on fire. At least I wasn't the only player suffering. Ian Woosnam missed the cut, lucky man, and Nick Faldo's returns featured two rounds in the 80s at a time when he was one of the world's best players. The entire field for the weekend action was no less than 563 over par.

The feeling in my limbs returned later that month in Madrid where a weekend 67–65 return hauled me into fourth – a position which produced some very welcome Ryder Cup points. The match was very much a part of my agenda for the season because I had thoroughly enjoyed my return to the Europe side in 1989 after an eight-year gap. Previously when I had played, the American team was so strong that the result was never in serious doubt, the crowds were small and consequently there was more atmosphere to be found at an Ilkley old folks' whist drive. But by 1989 the match had been transformed. It was no longer an exhibition, but an occasion, and one I wanted to be part of for as long as possible.

I would also have loved a more high-profile role in the American major championships, but the balance of opportunity was heavily weighted against Europeans. I was 36 before I received my first invitation to play in the US

Open. I felt there was something wrong in a system that placed me thirty-third in the world yet could only guarantee me a place in one of the four grand slam events. Top Europeans could not get in, but lesser-order Americans were often to be found winning either the US Open or PGA. Many from this side of the pond were restricted to the Open in Britain, and that was the hardest to win because it invariably had the strongest field. And if you didn't perform well on links then it was goodnight Vienna to your chances of ever winning a major.

The 1991 season quickly became a bit of a grind, not least because we invariably seemed to be playing in cold conditions, but the Open was back at Royal Birkdale in the summer so that was something to look forward to. Others would contend the top spots, though. I finished ten shots behind Australian Ian Baker-Finch – no disgrace, but another chance had passed and I was now nearer 40 than 30.

It was obvious when I missed the cut at the European Pro-Celebrity tournament at Hoylake in the second week of August that something was again desperately wrong with my game. Gavin Christie recommended more swing changes because he had noticed my takeaway had become a little narrow. More width would allow me to swing freely through the ball.

It was a fine diagnosis. A first-round 66 in my defence of the NM English Open title at the Belfry the following week included an inward 30. Those last nine holes were arguably the best I had played in my entire career and included six successive birdies. Unfortunately, there would be no repeat of it, and as the weeks went by it became increasingly more certain that if I was to be a part of the

Europe team to face America in Kiawah Island it would be by selection rather than my own efforts. And so it proved. Captain Bernard Gallacher went down the money list to twenty-second place to find me and put my name against a wild card. It was an enormous relief, yet although I felt I was worth my place I knew I had to show it because there had been many names above me in the list when the qualification period ended. I had been trying too hard and it had affected my game. I had tried not to let the pressure get to me, but with everybody talking about the Ryder Cup and asking me about it, it had proved difficult.

A slip from tenth to twenty-first in the rankings was the result of a year without a victory, but I was still in the top 40 in the world rankings, although that wasn't enough to win me an invitation to Augusta in 1992. The Royal & Ancient had tried to reflect global standings by inviting Europe's and America's top 20 to the Open along with the top 50 in the world rankings, but the Masters in Georgia remained a law unto themselves.

A rare missed cut at the Open at Muirfield that July was followed by the runner-up spot behind American Paul Azinger at the BMW International Open in Munich, but in general the 1992 season was one of mediocrity for me. My thirty-second place in the money list was my joint worst in seventeen years on Tour. Something had to be done. Something was.

14. EXOTIC TASTES

I have always enjoyed playing golf in the heat, both of the weather and the battle kind, and Madeira in January 1993 became the perfect place to start golf as a soon-to-be 40-year-old. The press had not been slow to point out that it had been three years since my last success. It was time to get rid of my new 'former winner' tag, and it was a surprise to be playing so well so early in the season after a long winter break. It was my first tournament since the beginning of the previous November, but I played solidly all week and held off the challenge of my English compatriots Gordon J. Brand and Paul Broadhurst to win by three.

After leading at the halfway stage in Tenerife shortly afterwards, I found myself with a new tag: 'the golfer who seems to thrive in tournaments on exotic islands'. I could just as easily have been dubbed the flyaway golfer because my clubs had failed to arrive with me on the plane from Heathrow and I had given them until Wednesday lunch-time to be delivered or I was booked on a flight back. They arrived just in time to stop me boarding the plane, and it was just as well because after going almost three years without a win I now had a second title inside a month. And, of course, I was already very handily placed in the Ryder Cup table as well as being top of the money list.

Madeira had been a pleasant surprise, but Tenerife had not shocked me in the slightest because I could hardly remember four successive rounds when I had struck the ball so consistently out of the middle of the bat. I hit every green in regulation in the last round which showed me that my nerve was still strong, and I was able to avoid putting any strain on my suspect putting by hitting many of my approach shots close.

One of the things I am sure helped me in those days was the knowledge that although I was heading into the back nine of my career, my game continued to improve. Although the best I ever played (if not scored) was the closing 65 that edged out American Ed Sneed by a shot in the 1979 Carroll's Irish Open, the Mark James of 1993 was infinitely more rounded. I had only been able to move the ball one way, left to right, in my earlier days, but now I felt comfortable over any shot. Name a flight path and I felt I could launch the ball on it. A lifetime spent standing over four-foot putts had taken a certain toll on my central nervous system, but I still felt comfortable under pressure and that came from keeping a clear mind and being aware of the pitfalls. I never looked two shots forward or back, I just took my time and stayed with what I did when I wasn't under pressure. The more I kept everything the same, the more likely I was to hit the shots I knew I could hit.

I hit more of that type of shot on my return to St Mellion for the Benson & Hedges. Following my millions over par in the arctic blasts of the previous year, I managed four sub-par rounds and ended up runner-up to Paul Broadhurst. All was well with my world, although I suffered a devastating blow at home at this time. I discovered I had planted my runner beans too early and the frost had got to them – a mistake I have not repeated since.

Though my game was in much better shape, I was convinced I had not even approached my full potential. But I had always been an average putter and there was no question that to reach the highest level you had to be at least better than average, bordering on good, in that department. I wasn't complaining, however, because I had achieved what I had set out to do in the first place and made a reasonable amount of money. I knew that to win majors I would have to hole a lot of putts, and I didn't. Neither did I save enough pars, but fate would decide and I would not be losing any shuteye over it because I could do no more than I had, and that was my best. If I ever sulked about a bad round, it lasted no more than ten seconds. I never took golf home with me, neither would I fret if I never won a major. I may not have reached the top of the game, but there are a lot of other golfers who would give anything for my career, never mind Jack Nicklaus's.

The Open at St George's would prove no different than recent previous ones, although a top-25 finish was not to be sniffed at. I never got anywhere near sniffing distance of the claret in the silver jug as Greg Norman finished two shots clear of Faldo to claim the second and last of his majors. Nevertheless, my conviction that 1992 had been no more than a downward blip on my career graph proved accurate as I moved back to eleventh in the Order of Merit by the end of 1993.

There was a certain irony in my turning down an invitation to play in the 1994 US Open because I had spent much of my career regretting that I got far too few opportunities to play in the three majors on American soil, but I was getting a little picky in my old age and at that stage I was happier playing on the links of Jersey than hacking out of the rough in Oakmont. A second-place finish in Jersey behind Paul Curry more or less justified my decision, at least in my own mind.

Nothing else that happened in the first half of 1994 gave me a great deal of hope going into Turnberry, but it was the Open, and I have never been anything other than totally motivated in the hunt for a sip out of the silver claret jug. It was a perfect day for scoring when the game's oldest championship got under way on the west coast of Scotland, but I failed to seize the opportunity, although an opening 72 would have suited more than half the field. There was a huge improvement in the second round with one of my best Open rounds, a 67, and there was even better to come, for a Saturday 66 put me just four shots behind Fuzzy Zoeller and Brad Faxon. The bookmakers were not as optimistic as I was, for I was quoted at 33–1, the same odds as Greg Norman, and he was two shots worse off. I figured I needed a 66 to have any kind of chance, but even a 64 would not have been good enough because Zimbabwe's Nick Price proved what a great player he is by forging ahead and pipping Sweden's Jesper Parnevik by just one stroke. My 68 took me to fourth, but coming down the stretch it was obvious the winner would be one of the two players who went on to finish first and second.

Price has always been a true gentleman of the game, and having come close behind Tom Watson at Troon in 1982 and Seve Ballesteros six years later at Lytham, few outside Sweden would have begrudged him his finest hour. 'Oh boy!' he said at the prizegiving ceremony. 'In 1982 I had my left hand on it; in 1988 I had my right hand on it; and now I have got both on it, and doesn't it feel good!' I'm sure it did. How I would have loved to have had that feeling.

I didn't feel at all good not long afterwards when I read Nick Faldo's criticisms of the European Tour. For the first and only time in my life I felt the need to go into the press centre to put my point of view. I was not a happy budgie, and I launched an attack on appearance money while advising the recipients to plan their schedules around venues rather than play-for-pay. I felt the top players already had more than enough money and should not be given extra inducements. I was also upset that Faldo felt our Tour was not making progress, and thought he wasn't exactly in the best position to pass comment when he was seldom playing in Europe. Faldo asked me to withdraw my criticisms, but I refused.

It wasn't the only time that season I would feel compelled to defend the Tour and the progress it had made under chief executive Ken Schofield and his team. Why they should be criticised for extending the Tour's boundaries to pastures beyond Europe defeated me, particularly early in the year when the weather was better elsewhere and everything else, from the standard of play to the standard of courses, followed suit. Our Tour members were truly international, so it was only common sense to have a truly international schedule.

My travels in 1994 were not exactly fruitful, however, but 1995 was Ryder Cup year again, further incentive to get things back on course. Key decisions had to be made, not least about my putting, and I made the quantum leap to the broom-handle putter. I had been putting no better than average for most of my nineteen years on Tour so there was nothing to lose and hopefully plenty to gain, although I felt something of a fraud, having been a traditionalist in my beliefs in this particular department. If I needed any convincing that this was the way forward, it came in March in the first tournament in which I used it.

The Moroccan Open at Royal Agadir marked the broom's debut, and four days later I was using it to acknowledge the applause that greeted my victory. Sam Torrance had pioneered the long putter in Europe, but I used a slightly different method. Whereas he tucked the putter under his chin, I got one that was slightly shorter so that I could anchor it more in my chest. It certainly made me feel safer and more solid, particularly over the dodgy lengths between five and eight feet. Eight birdies in the last round in Morocco were testimony to the method's efficiency.

My feelings for the Open far outweighed those for the venue for 1995, St Andrews again, but I managed to put together another top-ten finish behind John Daly. It was a real surprise on a course I don't particularly like, and with the wind blowing between 30 and 40mph as well. Actually, I think I produced the best last 36 holes, a 68 and a 70, to leapfrog into eighth. I was now starting to believe, however, that I was destined never to reach the top spot. At least I featured in another Ryder Cup, but I headed towards winter in serious need of a rest and some skiing rather than golf.

My attitude during the 1996 season was summed up best by my final standing in the Order of Merit. In twenty previous seasons I had never finished lower than thirty-second; this time I plummeted to position number 116, and there was neither excuse nor explanation for the poor standard of golf I had produced. I'd even had a little difficulty lifting myself for the Open, although my twenty-second place at Lytham behind Tom Lehman was one of my better finishes.

Lytham is probably the least aesthetically pleasing of all the Open courses because it's surrounded by houses, railway lines, newsagents, plumbers, electricians, Indian takeaways and the town in general, but to play there is a joy for it's a very, very good test. I have no problem starting with a par three because it gets play away; usually you're delayed out on the course rather than while you're practising putting. It is a bit out and in, but it does it with a little more variation than some courses. I think maybe the only stretch of holes in the same direction is the first three, and after that you do switch around a little bit. The last two holes are tough under any conditions, but they always seem tougher when it's the Open.

The 1996 season as a whole might have been one to forget, but those who wondered if this was the end of my career were forgetting one thing: another Ryder Cup was looming, and I intended to be part of it.

15. ACE HIGH

I gave myself every possible chance of being in the side that would compete in continental Europe for the first time with one of the most satisfying weeks of my entire career. Hungry for the game again after a mini-sabbatical the previous year, I entered the Spanish Open at La Moraleja in Madrid on 24 April armed with no great confidence after four missed cuts, but carrying a short putter, the broom-handle version having been dispensed to the broom cupboard at the start of the season. It turned into a battle of the over-40s as Greg Norman – at 42, one year my junior – chased me all the way into a not-so-sudden-death play-off after he birdied the last in regulation play and I dropped a shot. I needed three extra holes to secure my eighteenth win in Europe, but it was well worth the wait.

Success meant a huge amount to me because it gave me the confidence in my ability to carry on after I had started to doubt myself. It was not so much an age thing that had started to eat away at my self-assurance, rather the realisation that if you do lose it for a year or two there is less inclination to work your backside off to get it back. Now I knew exactly where I stood with myself and the game.

I'd put the Ryder Cup on the back burner because there were more imminent challenges, not least qualifying for the Open. After the Spanish, I added a top-ten finish at the English Open, then at the end of May I headed for Wentworth and the Volvo PGA Championship. I like Wentworth, but in 1997 it did not return my affection and

I missed the cut. Fortunately I had done enough to get one of the Open exemptions handed out to the top-five non-exempt players in the top twenty of the money list after the PGA.

Troon is another championship course I'm not exactly wild on. I don't really know why because it's a very good, straightforward links; I just don't like the feel of it, simple as that. Maybe it's because all the bunkers are in just the right place to catch my drives. It's undoubtedly a good course, and you can't knock its challenging aspects because it's long, tough and exposed to a wind that invariably adds to the difficulty. But it is straight out, straight in, and I've never been overly keen on courses that head you out in one direction and bring you straight back. I prefer a bit more variety and direction. I feel some of the others have that, but St Andrews and Troon are a wee bit mundane from that point of view.

Troon favours the long, straight hitter who strikes good irons and putts well, so that's probably why I have never done particularly well there. I think I finished in the top fifteen in 1989, and that's the only decent finish I've had in that particular corner of Scotland. I actually played really well that year because the course was quite bouncy and the rough was not too deep, so it played like a links. You definitely had to think your way round it and be very careful.

I had taken the hard route to the 1997 Open, and it got no easier once I got there because a first-round 76 meant I was staring at only my third missed cut in twenty seasons. My anxiety was eased by a 67 that took me into the top twenty, but that's where I remained, too far back ever to get into contention.

The season was memorable in other respects, though – not least for my first ever Tour hole-in-one at the Volvo German Open in June. I aced with a five-iron at the 194-yard eighth, but it was typical of the way things had been going for me that I chose the wrong hole. Had I holed out at the seventeenth, I would have won a £20,000 car; all I got on the eighth were the congratulations of my playing partners Ian Woosnam and Sven Struver. At least I moved up 102 places in the Order of Merit, back into the top twenty, though not high enough at the right time to get me into Seve Ballesteros's Ryder Cup team for Valderrama.

The trend in my career graph since 1990 showed that I always played better in odd-numbered years. It was no coincidence that those years were Ryder Cup years. The trend continued right through the decade, too: I had dropped to fifty-eighth in the standings in 1998, but came back in 1999 to collect more than £300,000 in prize money for only the second time.

The irony of the 1999 season, when I would in fact win more money than in any other year at the ripe old age of 46, was that I came to the last event of the Ryder Cup counting programme with a very good chance of making the team. Soon after my appointment to the captaincy, Tour chief Ken Schofield had approached me and said, 'Congratulations, Captain. If you get in, you'll play, of course?' 'Absolutely,' I replied, although at the time I considered it unlikely. No way could I have considered both playing and captaining, those days were long gone, but press speculation about whether I would or not was rife throughout the entire season because I never once made my views known publicly. It was an intentional ploy.

Had I said I would definitely be playing if I made the team then they would have been trying to guess my replacement as captain, and that would not have been fair on anybody, particularly Ken Brown, who was ready to take over the reins and would have received all the aggravation of the job but possibly without actually captaining the side.

At the start of 1999 I had very few reasons to believe that I would have any chance at all of getting into the top ten because my form in 1998 had bordered on abysmal at times and I had seen nothing to suggest it was going to change. When I headed towards South Africa that winter, I had no idea what to expect – apart from decent weather and food. Making the cut was something of a result at the time, but I was still in a state of uncertainty in February 1999 when I arrived in Dubai for my debut on the European season. Such are the vagaries of this most frustrating yet rewarding of games that I suddenly started making contact with the ball better than I had for a long time. I finished third in the desert, and a month later went one better in Madeira.

There was still a suspicion that my form was suspect because Dubai was only my second event of the year, and I had finished the previous season with my arm in a sling after tearing a shoulder muscle during the Volvo Masters. I hadn't practised until the middle of January. My misgivings were not misplaced. I was starting to show Ryder Cup form, but just as soon as it arrived, away it disappeared, faster than Tiger Woods's clubhead. I was still wondering what had happened at the end of May when I arrived at Wentworth for the Volvo PGA Championship, not an event or venue for discovering form because you need to attack the West Course with your game finely honed. Just as quickly as it had come and gone, lo and behold, my game returned. I finished second to Colin Montgomerie, a result that not only swelled the James bank balance by some £145,000 – more than my total earnings for my first six years on Tour – but also put me seventh on the Ryder Cup money list with stacks of counting events still to come.

I knew that if I changed my schedule and played more, there was every possibility I would make the team, but there was also the distinct chance that I would be over-golfed and therefore not much use to them. So I stuck to my schedule, and to my guns: I would not play and be captain because I was sure it was tough enough to be captain and just to keep breathing normally, let alone play as well.

The Open at Carnoustie was a strange affair to say the least, and although I played all four rounds not one of them was less than a 74. The head greenkeeper came in for plenty of stick for the way the course had been set up – tight, fast fairways and rough as high as an elephant's eye – but there were certainly no shortcomings in the last-hole drama department.

France's Jean Van de Velde, whose performance almost guaranteed him a Ryder Cup place, became the most celebrated runner-up in Open history by taking seven at the last when a double-bogey six would have made him the champion. The picture of him paddling in the greenside burn went round the world a thousand times, while Scotland's Paul Lawrie became the local hero, coming from ten shots back in the last round to win in a play-off. That said much for Paul's fortitude and nerve because he also had to account for former champion Justin

Leonard in overtime, and he did so with the steel and determination that would serve him so well in Brookline three months later.

Carnoustie is nothing less than a great course, but I think they tightened it up too much in 1999. There were a couple of holes – one in particular, the par-five sixth – where you had only about ten yards to hit it in, and that's too narrow a target from way out. The biggest problem, however, was that it didn't seem to have the depth of turf most links courses have, so it was more like a motorway. It became something of a lottery when you hit a five-iron off the tee and saw your ball travel 250 yards. Even for a links it got a little too firm, but having said that, it's normally a great test of golf. It's long and tight, and the bunkers are well positioned, even if some are becoming redundant, though new technology doesn't seem to have affected Carnoustie as much as other courses. It's just too relentless, and of course the last three holes can be incredibly tough. The par-three sixteenth can demand a driver into the wind. At a recent Dunhill Links Championship I hit a driver there and it didn't reach. If the seventeenth is into the wind, it's two big hits, while if it's downwind you've got somehow to feather it into the gap between the two burns, and that's far from easy. And then you get to eighteen – just a massive minefield of a par four.

I had a lot of sympathy for Van de Velde's experience; it was tragic that he didn't win. He had done everything you could ask of a player for 71 holes, and I could see his thinking going up the last. The one mistake he made was with his third shot. He had to make sure he got his third shot over the burn. I could understand him hitting a driver off the tee and going for the second shot, that's exactly what I would have done had I been fortunate enough to be in that situation, but it was the third shot that proved his undoing. He did have options. Having had that nightmare bounce back off the stand with his second shot, the preferred one should have been to take a drop and be left with a 70- to 80-yard pitch. It was a great shame that he didn't win because he deserved to, but having said that I think Paul's last round and play-off were stunning, and no credit should be taken away from him.

My own form after Carnoustie gradually disintegrated again on the back of another stretch of woeful putting – the fault of the puttee, not the putter – and I was fast running out of Ryder Cup counting events. Not that that was particularly annoying because I was definitely going as captain, and that was something I wanted to do. I scraped together a few points at the US PGA Championship at Medinah, then went to Germany towards the end of August needing to finish no lower than second at the BMW International. Not until well into the last day of that tournament did it become obvious that come autumn in Boston I would for the first time be leading the players out in a Ryder Cup.

16. (NOT SO) EASY RYDER

The Ryder Cup was something I was aware of rather than particularly interested in when I set out on my professional career in the mid-1970s. That ambivalence probably stemmed from the fact that every time we played it we used to get our backsides well and truly kicked by Uncle Sam's spikes. The biennial match, though, would become a passion for me – not all-consuming, but definitely an event to be treasured, respected and looked forward to in the golfing calendar. Sam Ryder's legacy to the game became something I wanted to play, and now I believe it is an event pretty much all European players seriously want to be involved with.

There are three ways of ranking players' success through their careers: there are major championship winners, there are Ryder Cup players and there are tournament winners. Major winners in Europe are few and far between, but tournament winners are fairly plentiful, so to be a Ryder Cup player is to be a cut above a tournament winner and one step down from a grand slam title holder. I think that's why everyone is so keen to play for Europe. Another reason now, of course, is that it is such a huge honour to represent your Tour. It is something everyone wants to experience, and the fact that it's held just once every two years makes it that bit more exclusive. It's not like playing cricket or football for England with a number of matches every year. The Ryder Cup is an infrequent and colossal event.

I have never been big on setting targets or goals for the simple reason that if you do and you attain them, you may get complacent. Conversely, if you do have an agenda and do not see it through, you could become disappointed to the extent that frustration sets in. When that happens, your game tends to go out of the locker-room window. But I always made an exception with the Ryder Cup. It was a must-do thing.

It was more by default than design that I got into the 1977 team because I finished outside the standings at the end of the qualification system, but something or somebody persuaded captain Brian Huggett, or whoever selected the wild cards then, to pick me. I had finished eleventh on the list so it was hardly a controversial choice, but I was still somewhat surprised if pleased to be deemed good enough to face the might of America. It would be the last time Great Britain and Ireland went into battle without the assistance of Europe.

The number of matches had been cut from 32 to 20 in the hope of giving us a better chance, but, to be brutally honest, in those days they could have reduced them to any number and we would still have gone in as underdogs. We went to the first tee at Royal Lytham & St Annes hoping to do well, the Americans entered the fray expecting to win. That had very much been the historical routine of the competition, and nothing much happened in Lancashire that September to alter the course of normal proceedings. My baptism in the 12½–7½ defeat was not so much one of fire as inferno. I partnered Tommy Horton against no less a double act than Jack Nicklaus and Tom Watson. We played out of our skins and restricted them to a 5 & 4 success, but I don't remember being particularly nervous – a trait that would stay with me over the years.

The 1977 match was altogether different to the way it is today because there were few rules and restrictions and just as many spectators. It was not so much a match as an exhibition, and it was the Americans who did most of the exhibiting while we tended to make an exhibition of ourselves. There was no great feeling of team spirit, no team room as such, and if you wanted to go for a walk – or even to a nightclub, as my teetotal pal Ken Brown, Eamonn Darcy, Jane and I did one night – nobody raised so much as an eyebrow.

All sorts of objections and accusations were thrown at Ken and I two years later at the Greenbrier in West Virginia. It has to be admitted that we didn't give much for anybody's feelings about us at that time. We were in a society where senior golfers expected to be respected simply because they were senior to us or had won a few titles. We were young and of the opinion that people had to earn our respect, and consequently we were labelled rebels, although for the life of me I cannot think what our cause was, if we had one. Our only aspirations were to be the best players we possibly could be while winning as much money as we could to ensure that we never had to get a proper job, but at the time it did seem that trouble was a middle name we shared. We often had to chuck our hard-earned pennies into the Tour's fine fund, and after the Ryder Cup clash we were firmly in place as its greatest ever contributors. Prior to that, the most I had had to cough up was the odd £20 for throwing a club, swearing or general non-conformation to accepted standards of behaviour. Certainly less than £1,000 in total.

Those incidents at the Greenbrier have been well catalogued; suffice it to say here that if anything could have gone wrong, it did, and when it did Ken and I could not have been more centre-stage had we been moved a millimetre in any direction. The worst part for me was ripping a rib cartilage while taking my luggage off the carousel on arrival in the USA, and after the first morning's fourballs I took no further part in the match. However, according to the list of alleged misdemeanours I took part in plenty of them, most of them unsavoury in the eyes of officialdom.

Shortly after we returned home from the 17–11 drubbing, Ken and I were summoned to appear before a meeting of the Tour Committee that attracted a record attendance. Unfortunately it clashed with an episode of *Star Trek*, so 40 minutes after arriving at the appointed hour and not having been called, I was on my way home, leaving Ken to face the music alone. I eventually appeared about a month later, pleaded 'untrue' to about eighteen counts and 'true' to the heinous crime of writing '(s.o.b.)' after Sandy Lyle's name on one of the official menus. My case was not helped by the fact that this particular *carte du jour* belonged to a vicar. I have to admit that my actions were well out of order in this instance and I probably did deserve some kind of punishment.

I knew beforehand they were going to throw the book at me, and I had to throw my chequebook at them. They withdrew my match fee of £1,000 and slapped another £500 fine on top to create a new British, Commonwealth, all-comers and probably world record. The irony of the situation was that had I been that bad in 1979 there was no way I would have been selected for the 1981 match by continuing captain John Jacobs, but I was, which led me to the conclusion that there had been forces at work determined to nail me.

We were still getting nailed on the course, too. The matches weren't getting much closer at all, despite the appearance of several top Europeans on the team. The duel at Walton Heath was as memorable for events off the course as those on it, in particular the controversial non-selection of Seve Ballesteros, even though he was our best player at the time. The Spaniard had been one of the European pioneers two years earlier and was now a genuine superstar with two grand slam titles already in the trophy cabinet.

Seve had not qualified for the team automatically and at that time was basically holding the Tour to ransom over appearance money. The players felt it wrong that one player should be trying for and often succeeding in getting so much money when the proceeds of the tournament were not really that big. Seve was refusing to play unless he was paid large sums. He actually played only seven events in 1981, even though he finished seventh on the money list. The feeling among the players was very much that they weren't all that keen on having him on the team, and John Jacobs and his co-selectors Bernhard Langer, who was leading the points table, and Neil Coles, chairman of the tournament committee, did not give him a wild card. The Spaniard's omission naturally caused quite a stir, and he was not best pleased with the Tour. I don't think he and Ken Schofield, the Tour's executive director, ever really saw eye to eye after that.

Appearance money – I only ever received it once during my career, and it was a fairly insignificant amount – has always been a contentious issue. Large sums can be incredibly detrimental to the Tour, but quite often it's the only way to keep some tournaments going. If the prize fund is relatively small or the tournament is a bit out of the way, then the only way sometimes to attract the top players is to give them some kind of fiscal inducement. Although appearance money *per se* is something that is perceived as unnecessary, unwanted and damaging, certainly during the late 1970s some of the continental tournaments were kept going by Mark McCormack's International Management Group. Had there not been one or two stars appearing in some events they would simply have folded.

Nowadays we hear tales of how Tiger Woods gets huge sums of money, into the millions of dollars, to play in tournaments, but if it means he comes over to play in the TPC in Germany, then why not? The prize fund is $3 million and it's one of our biggest tournaments, so we're happy, the sponsors are happy and Tiger is probably happy. Under those circumstances it's difficult to find anyone who isn't happy. The problems really only occur these days when you have a relatively small tournament and someone is getting a vast appearance fee. That happened, I think, at the 2002 New Zealand Open. Tiger's appearance fee was reputed to be £1.5 million, yet the prize purse was only £300,000. All hell broke loose. Prices for admission were said to be going up 1,000 per cent, and the players were distinctly unhappy – in particular Greg Turner, a Kiwi but long-time campaigner on the European Tour, who started waging a one-man lobby. He fought for the entrance fees to be significantly reduced, and eventually they were.

Back in the 1980s it was the likes of Seve Ballesteros, Nick Faldo, Bernhard Langer, Sandy Lyle and Ian Woosnam, Europe's Big Five, who very much controlled the appearance-money market until the arrival of the newer players in the 1990s, the likes of Lee Westwood and

Darren Clarke. These two particularly are to be applauded for their stance against receiving inducements, as long as nobody else was, but the wishes of the sponsors to get a number of top players to tournaments meant that several players were frequently paid – not necessarily appearance money, but certainly carrots by way of a pre-tournament jamboree in the form of a shoot-out or an exhibition, or lunch with the sponsors.

The Tour has tried to keep such things under strict control so that fees do not exceed prize funds, and in general it has succeeded, but when a player of Tiger's stature comes on the scene it quickly becomes impossible to control sweeteners. Some would argue, quite rightly, that he brings something to a tournament that no one else in the world can at the moment. I think the good he has done to the game of golf is similar to that of Jack Nicklaus and Arnold Palmer in the 1960s. He has brought, as they did, a whole new generation of golfers into the sport.

In the early 1980s my fortunes, of the playing variety, within the Ryder Cup team structure began to improve. I played alongside the not inconsiderable presence of Sandy Lyle twice in 1981 and we won both matches on the first day, against Bill Rogers and Bruce Lietzke in the morning foursomes and Ben Crenshaw and Jerry Pate in the afternoon fourballs. We gelled really well. I have always liked Sandy for he's an uncomplicated chap, dead easy to get on with. His massive hitting was foiled nicely by my mishits, and in fact the team went into the second day holding a 4½–3½ lead, but that was pretty much it. The Americans had assembled essentially a dream team that had the best of the old, players like Lee Trevino and Jack Nicklaus, with the best of the new, players like Jerry Pate and Bill Rogers, who had just won the Open at Royal St George's. They had looked extremely strong on paper, and unfortunately for us they proved just as strong on grass. We won just four more matches during the rest of the week to earn five points out of the last twenty. The result, 18½–9½, was not a pretty picture for Europe, but that was the final drubbing to date America has inflicted on us.

I missed the next three Ryder Cups, the period of the European renaissance. While I was busy trying to effect a renaissance with my own game, the rest of the Tour was doing brilliantly. Europe started to sprout claws capable of damaging American pride in 1983, and we gave them a hell of a fright at Palm Beach Gardens in Florida. Although we lost, it was only by one point, and things could so easily have gone our way. It was a wake-up call the Americans had still not responded to two years later, when the match went to the Belfry for the first time.

There was a hint of what was to follow after the morning foursomes – our history in this particular discipline is far more suspect than many people realise – because despite Seve Ballesteros and Manuel Pinero giving us a point from the first match, the other three went to the boys in the stars and stripes. But we edged the afternoon fourballs and were just a point back come the end of the first day.

The glorious uncertainty of golf was never better highlighted than on the second morning. Ballesteros and Pinero were our only losers, and we even managed a 3–1 success in the afternoon foursomes to give us a 9–7 lead going into the last-day singles – another discipline that had not been particularly kind to us over the years. But 1985 was not any old year, it was destined to stay indelibly in the mind, particularly Sam Torrance's. For much of the last day, it was not so much a case of if we would claim an historic victory, but where. Sam gave us the answer on the last green when he raised his arms in a perfect 'V for Victory' salute to acknowledge his triumph over double US Open champion Andy North, sealing Europe's first win in 28 years.

If that was a victory to remember, the one in 1987 was one to savour, nothing short of an incredible performance as Europe won on American soil for the first time against a US team captained by Jack Nicklaus and playing on his magnificent Muirfield Village course. It was the year when the likes of Faldo and Woosnam, Ballesteros and Olázabal, and Lyle and Langer seemed virtually unbeatable. Captain Tony Jacklin said he'd never thought he would live to see the day when golf of that standard was produced. The six players were absolutely at their peak. Woosnam was without doubt the best striker in the world at that period. Faldo had just got his game back together and won the Open at Muirfield, while Olázabal hit the Tour running and was obviously a genius. Seve was still at his peak, and Sandy had won the Open two years earlier and would win the Masters the following year. He was nothing short of tremendous, and Langer was right at the top of his game as well. Those six really did play some fantastic stuff. I would have loved to have been there, but my time in America would come.

I think 1987 at Muirfield Village was a huge turning point for the European Tour. Suddenly we had become competitive with the States, for although we won in 1985 I felt they had a relatively poor team none of whose members was playing particularly well. That in itself was incredible, because it was only four years after 1981, when they had had such a good outfit. They had a decent team in 1987, but ours was just fantastic.

The reasons for my absence in the mid-1980s had everything to do with form and nothing to do with lack of desire. I wanted to be there, I just wasn't good enough. I played reasonably well in 1985 and finished fourteenth on the money list, pretty close to making the team automatically. It was my only route there because I had a good idea that the wild cards would be winging their way into letterboxes other than mine. There was really not an awful lot wrong with my game, but in 1986 I started to play very, very badly, a run of awful form which continued into 1987. I had just run into technical problems, exacerbated by my poor putting. My game just disappeared, simple as that. At the end of 1987 and start of 1988 I packed the game in for a few months and got out the previously mentioned ciné films.

I started to play some extremely good stuff in 1988, striking the ball well the whole season. I would say that for four or five years, through to about 1993, I was almost as good as Ian Woosnam in Europe and certainly among the top three strikers at that time. I played exceptionally well, hitting the ball very straight and finding a lot of greens in regulation. My bad shots were few and far between, and that always makes the game easier. My putting slowly started to edge back too, simply because there was less pressure on it.

It was my successful reappearance in 1988 that triggered this run, although again it was not without incident. I became probably the only player in history ever to sack his caddie after a win. After that Spanish Open triumph I finished second in the PGA, but he still had to go. But then, he had set my bag on fire. During that Spanish Open in Santander he had brought to the course a big woolly 'Hogan' bag strap cover to make things more comfortable for himself. I couldn't have a Hogan strap on my bag because I was contracted to Ping, so he spent two days unpicking the offending name woven into it, then on the third day he left his pipe resting against the bag and set it on fire. His days were numbered from that point.

My Ryder Cup days were about to start their own countdown in 1989, and I continued to play really well, winning three tournaments and losing in a play-off for another. I was really on top of my game and comfortably qualified for the European team that was now seeking a hat-trick of victories at the Belfry.

I was paired with Howard Clark for the first day, and that was perfectly fine by me, although I had suspected he might have been better off with Ronan Rafferty because at that time they used the same ball. But Howard is a good friend, a good player and reliable under pressure, which is the sort of partner I always like. We lost the first one to Lanny Wadkins and Payne Stewart, but then in the afternoon we beat Fred Couples and Wadkins before being rested for the Saturday morning foursomes. We were reunited for the afternoon fourballs and accounted for Stewart and Curtis Strange.

My roll continued in the singles where I prevailed over Mark O'Meara 3 & 2, and that gave me three points out of four – without doubt my best result in a Ryder Cup. But the occasion was soured a little for me because we failed to beat the Americans. We may have retained the trophy after a 14–14 draw, but considering we were in a situation where we couldn't lose I don't think we went out on to the course to bring in the others in sufficient numbers. The last four all lost, and what could have been a glorious day was just a good enough one. I don't really know what came over everyone, but it was the captain's job to make sure some people were out there watching the last few matches coming in.

Kiawah Island in 1991 was also a disappointment, not least because it was inappropriately dubbed the 'War on the Shore' as it followed shortly after the Gulf War in which we had fought alongside the Americans. A lot was said about crowd reaction there, but I never found it too bad, although I suspect I missed the worst of it. Whatever happened certainly paled into insignificance when compared to the events at Brookline eight years later.

The unfortunate thing about Kiawah is that history will remember it as the Ryder Cup decided by Bernhard Langer's missed seven-foot putt on the last green. The competition is about teams not individuals, and nobody in our locker room placed any blame whatsoever on the German's broad shoulders. Indeed, had a vote been taken among our players as to who we would have wanted standing over a putt to win the Ryder Cup, I'm fairly certain Bernhard's name would have been top of the list. The way he threw back his head and contorted his face when the ball stayed out said much about how much it meant to him, but he had done brilliantly anyway to get himself into a position where he could affect the outcome. Just one point separated the teams again, which says everything about the way in which the nature of the match had changed over the years. Since Europe's 1981 hammering there has never been more than two points in it come the end.

The 1993 encounter, again at the Belfry, was a hard match, particularly as we had put ourselves in a perfect position to regain the trophy only to watch Tom Watson's team keep their hands on it with a late surge in the singles. Wins by Colin Montgomerie, Peter Baker and Joakim Haeggman high up the order gave us the perfect platform, but Messrs James, Rocca, Ballesteros, Olázabal and Langer could not muster a point between them, and the Ryder Cup flew west again.

It had been eighteen years since my Ryder Cup debut by the time we arrived in America for the 1995 encounter at Oak Hill and I had still to taste victory. Things were not easy for either me or Howard Clark because although we were paired on the first morning – beaten comprehensively by a majestic Davis Love and Jeff Maggert – our services were not called upon again until the final day's singles. Neither of us was playing particularly badly, but we just didn't get a chance to get into the line-up again.

I had no particular problem with that. If the captain sees it that way, then you have to go with it. It was Bernard Gallacher's decision, and he wanted to give us a chance to work on our game, but it's a long time to do that from Friday morning until Sunday afternoon. When I didn't play three players in 1999 for the first two days, I consequently knew a little bit about what it would be like for them. It is not easy. You play a few holes, practise, play a few holes, go out and support, practise a bit more, get up the next morning, play a few holes, go out and support, have lunch, practise, play a few holes – it really is as dull and as difficult as that. I think in 1995 Howard in particular found it tough, so for him to go out second in the singles behind Seve and win by one hole against Peter

Jacobsen was a great triumph. Of course he holed in one along the way, the second of the week for Europe following Costantino Rocca's at the fifth.

I went into bat at three against Jeff Maggert, and it proved to be the zenith of my long career as a mediocre putter. I holed a good few six-footers and put the ball close from 45 feet on several occasions on greens that were, at their slowest, swift. I was a couple under, and I don't think there were many people better than that all day. Oak Hill was a tough course and I felt I did well to beat Maggert 4 & 3. All you can do in a situation like that is play a good round. Sometimes you win, sometimes you lose, but you know if you go out and play well your captain cannot expect any more of you.

Winning on American soil was a truly wonderful experience and there was a fantastic atmosphere before, during and after. There were no crowd problems at all, even though we had been warned beforehand that there might be. Possibly we took them by surprise because we were behind and then suddenly came through quickly to take the trophy. It just didn't get any better than that.

Oak Hill was my final Ryder Cup as a player, but far from my last experience of it. I was an assistant to Seve Ballesteros in Valderrama in 1997, although not a million miles away from making the team under my own steam. It was a strange experience, for Seve is a unique character. After the first day I wasn't allowed in the team room, for whatever reason, though I would like to nail the myth here and now that it had anything to do with Nick Faldo. I tried to find out on the Sunday evening after the match was over, and both Nick and Seve assured me it was nothing to do with me. I know they were being honest. It was a strange situation, though, because Jane and I would mix with the players in the hotel bar prior to dinner before going one way to eat while they went another. Despite this bizarre set-up, I did my best to assist Seve.

Next time round it was my turn, though I hadn't given much thought to the possibility of being captain until after the 1997 match. Sam Torrance and I came to the same conclusion: there really were no real contenders apart from the two of us, and we still had our careers to think about. Because neither of us had given up hope of playing in the next team, we managed to persuade the committee to hang fire on an appointment until the summer of 1998, by which time we would have a decent idea which one of us had the better chance of qualifying. When decision time came it looked as though Sam would have by far the better chance of making it as a player – although ultimately that would not prove to be the case – and I got the nod while he came to Brookline as an invaluable assistant.

The final chapter in my Ryder Cup career to date revolved around events during that match in Brookline: my controversial (although I didn't see it that way) decision to rest Jean Van de Velde, Andrew Coltart and Jarmo Sandelin until the final series of singles; America's marvellous fightback to recover from a four-point deficit going into the last day; and the despicable behaviour of some Americans both inside and outside the ropes. What happened in Boston was one of the reasons why I wrote *Into the Bear Pit*, but I also penned it for the Ryder Cup Committee, making a series of recommendations I considered necessary to save the competition. I have no idea what action, if any, is going to be taken because I haven't received a reply, or even an acknowledgement that they were in receipt of my missive. Possibly they were too busy trying to think of ways of removing me as a vice-captain of Sam's. Who knows? Having to resign from the 2001 Ryder Cup set-up may well have been truly my last involvement in the Ryder Cup – or could there be a last, strange twist to the story of my involvement in team golf's greatest competition?

Apart from having to make wild-card selections – arguably the worst thing I have ever had to do in my professional life – and one or two unsavoury last-day incidents at Brookline, I thoroughly enjoyed being captain. I had played in seven Ryder Cups and been an assistant in another, so I had had plenty of opportunities to see captains in operation, although it's difficult to learn from the Americans because you see very little of them and obviously they're not going to chat about methods with a member of the opposition. Your own captains are slightly different because you do talk to them, and after you've been there a few times they want to talk to you more too. I really don't think there's a better way to prepare for Ryder Cup captaincy than having been in a team yourself and soaking up the experience.

My first captain was Brian Huggett, and I thought he was brilliant: decisive, and not frightened of the super-stars. I remember one occasion when he gave Tony Jacklin a piece of his mind when our star turn hadn't seemed too keen to venture out on to the course to support other matches. All the players respected Huggett, and although we got fairly well beaten, I felt he did a good job in 1977. I don't think a captain should ever be measured in terms of how well his team fares.

Captains have different styles, and John Jacobs in 1979 and 1981 could not have been more diametrically opposed to Brian. John was far more easy-going and relaxed, whereas Huggett would urge you to 'Get stuck in, boys! I want you to knock them into the middle of next week!' John was more of a 'Play well and I'll see you for a cup of tea later' type of captain, but I enjoyed being in both their teams. You can never be too sure what style of captaincy will work, or even, if the team wins, whether or not the captain was responsible for it. You only have to go back to 1997 with Seve. He was heavily criticised by members of his team and the press, yet we won.

I never really got on particularly well with Tony Jacklin. I respected what he had achieved as a player, and there was certainly no question of my not playing with whoever he wanted me to play with, or saying I didn't want to play in a certain set of matches under him, as some players have done. I have never understood the type of player who tells a captain he doesn't want to play in fourballs or foursomes. I think you play all your career for occasions like the Ryder Cup and if your captain wants you to go out and play, not go out and play or hang from the balcony by your fingernails for a couple of hours, you should go out and do it.

Jacklin was captain of Europe four times, but I only played under him once and that was in 1989 when I wasn't particularly impressed by his decision-making. He had done a brilliant job in elevating the team and the competition during the mid-1980s, but my experience of him in the team room was that he would only have his ear bent by Seve or Nick – the superstar stratum of the team. On the whole I found him dictatorial. Having said that, though, he did win twice and retained the trophy once, and it's pretty difficult to argue with a record like that.

Jacklin was succeeded by his deputy Bernard Gallacher, who was probably nearer to my style of captaincy than the others. I could always see where Bernard was coming from, and I always felt he said things with the right amount of force. He was unlucky in 1991, when the match was decided on the last putt, and in 1993, when we went into the singles one point ahead and it was incredibly close again. It would have been tragic had he ended his tenure as captain without a win, but his day came at Oak Hill in 1995.

Bernard hadn't wanted to continue after 1993, but I think the players did genuinely want him to do it again. None of the more experienced players were ready to hang up their spikes to do the job, and everyone felt the Wentworth-based Scot had done a good job in 1991 and 1993. He got on well with all the players, even though he didn't play as regularly on the Tour, and he seemed to get on pretty well with those he didn't know. He was the right man for the job at the time, so it was only justice that he got his just rewards.

Come 1999, after my stint as Seve's assistant in Spain, it was my turn to prove my worth.

17. BROUGHT TO BOOK

My Ryder Cup career may have ended as a player in 1995, but the competition continued to dominate my professional life on and off the course, and never more so than in the spring and summer of 2000.

The serialisation of *Into the Bear Pit*, my account of events leading up to, during and after the 1999 Ryder Cup in Boston, started in May 2000 during the week of the PGA Championship at Wentworth. The tome, for reasons I could not fully understand in the overall context, seemed to rattle a few cages, not least those of some of the press corps. I had always considered the book to be a fair, honest and balanced account, but some people, including players and several sections of the Fourth Estate, seemed very keen to base their opinion of it on the serialisation alone. It was a mistake some would regret and later apologise for.

The press were waiting at the end of the Burma Road to grill me after the final round, and things quickly evolved into a situation where some of the press were heavily in agreement with Nick Faldo's argument and some were just as strongly on my side.

But it seemed that I was being accused of a transgression of Tour regulations, and my view at the time, and it still is my view, was that if I was guilty Faldo could have faced similar charges a number of times over the years.

The irony of the situation was that initially I had not wanted to talk about Faldo at length or in depth in the book, but he had caused such a furore in the last counting events in 1999 when I was captain, and had also spoken out in far from complimentary terms about my key player Colin Montgomerie, that I had to mention him more than I would have liked. Put simply, what he said and did was very much a part of the build-up to Brookline.

People who have read the book since have confessed that they're not sure what all the fuss was about, but the headline writer for the *Daily Mail*, the newspaper that serialised *Into the Bear Pit*, certainly created a stir with his work. Extracts were carefully chosen and it was made to seem that I had been wholly critical of Faldo, but there are a number of favourable comments about him in the book as well. I felt it was nothing if not fair, but obviously others disagreed – at least before they had read it.

For example, Lewine Mair, the golf correspondent of the *Daily Telegraph*, chose the word 'scurrilous' to describe what she obviously considered an attack on Faldo, although which passages she found 'grossly or obscenely abusive or defamatory' were never clearly identified, and in any case the book was not on general release at the time. Her observations must have been based purely on the serialisation, or perhaps she had read a different book. Whatever the truth of the matter – and it may have been a case of never let the facts interfere with a good story – there was nothing in *Into the Bear Pit* that matched her description. Still, 'scurrilous' was a word she would use again.

David Davies, in the *Guardian*, was far more rounded in a commentary column that appeared under the headline JAMES CAUGHT OUT FOR SAYING TOO LITTLE. He seemed to grasp the situation far better than some of his colleagues:

Two men, embittered by recent Ryder Cup experiences, are leading a petty and puerile campaign to try to force Mark James, the last captain of the European team and the current vice-captain, to resign. An unholy and unlikely alliance has been struck up by Nick Faldo, a former champion and dedicated loner, and Jean Van de Velde, celebrated for not being a champion, but gregarious almost to a fault.

Both men claim James should go because of the contents of a book, *Into the Bear Pit*, that came out under his name although written by the *Daily Express* journalist Martin Hardy. In it, James addresses the events at Brookline, in Boston, in the 1999 Ryder Cup and expresses interesting opinions on things that happened before and after the match.

Faldo and Van de Velde have their reasons for being upset, albeit none that justify their subsequent actions. Faldo, who seems to think he has a divine right to be in the Ryder Cup team after playing on 11 successive occasions, simply could not believe he had been left out last time and, pride punctured, has reacted viciously. Van de Velde, who got into the team on the back of his second place at the Open at Carnoustie, was then not played until the final singles series. He seems to feel this impugns his character in some way, clearly having no grasp of the concept of golf as a team game. James, tactically astute, built up a four-point lead going into the singles, an advantage any captain would kill for.

Both men, in furtherance of their campaign, have courted the press assiduously with the result that a full-scale trial by tabloid is now underway. The *Sun*, true to form, has mounted its own campaign to 'give James the elbow', but the *Daily Mail*, which bought serialisation rights of the book and then stirred up the whole distasteful affair with its sensationalised approach to some unexceptional incidents, now seems to be backing James.

It is, in fact, the *Mail*'s treatment of the serialisation that is the cause of the problem. Having won the bidding battle for the book, it then had to justify the expenditure by extracting as many of the 'best' bits that it could find. The trouble was, there were not that many, which is why the author's employer, the *Daily Express*, was outbid. Extracts had to be dressed up with huge headlines and spread across two pages to convince readers they were getting something exciting.

One effort, for instance, revealed the astonishing news that Colin Montgomerie had asked that a non-team member be asked to leave the team room. Wow! Gosh! Really? Another revealed that a good-luck letter to the team from Faldo had been binned – on the face of it a good tale, but the European team had agreed unanimously it should not be displayed on the notice board. It was a nice bit of tittle-tattle, but no more.

One of the problems of this kind of sensationalism is that people take away an impression based on the treatment of the story, rather than the story itself. Any sensible reading of the extracts would reveal that James brought a reasonable and balanced view to the proceedings, particularly when dealing with what has to be done to prevent a repetition of the Americans' appalling behaviour at Brookline.

Unfortunately, some of Fleet Street's finest, the Sunday paper columnists, spotted the buzz words 'fury' and 'rage', saw in James an easy target and started spouting about how the vice-captain must go for 'revealing secrets of the team room'. What secrets? Scour the book and there is nothing revealing or embarrassing from the team room.

Recently, a journalist proponent of James resigning said: 'Well, he only wrote it for the money. He said so.' And so he did. He admitted he had been told he could make 'a few bob out of it'. But he added that he had things he wanted to get off his chest with regard to the future of the Ryder Cup, important things that needed to be done if the Boston Bear Pit was not to be repeated. The journalist had indulged in selective listening.

This has been a sad and demeaning affair out of which James deserves to emerge not just with credit, but with his position as vice-captain for the 2001 match secure.

Unfortunately, that last sentiment would not be realised for reasons that said more about the people who made the decision than the circumstances surrounding it.

Sports writer Alan Fraser, in a column in the *Daily Mail*, called on all sides to show their true colours:

Nick Faldo unwittingly revealed the truth of the situation when he added this rider to his claim that players had been phoning him about the Mark James affair. 'That has not happened before,' said Faldo. Nor will it happen again, one is tempted to suggest. Faldo chatting with his fellow professionals is not easy to picture, considering his tendency to ignore his peers when he was on a single-minded march towards becoming a champion. As a prominent member of the European Tour said yesterday: 'I doubt if there are three players who have his telephone number.'

The signs are that Faldo is suffering from all the signs of 'phantom support' – early-morning phone calls and a strong desire to eat everything but humble pie. Even the officer leading the Light Brigade would be reluctant to charge with only Jean Van de Velde, Paul McGinley and Mickey Walker mounted and ready for battle.

Which is why Sam Torrance should not be so hesitant in demonstrating his full support for James as his nominated vice-captain. And he should do it now. The Ryder Cup captain has been playing a waiting game, full of the kind of stalling statements and delaying tactics that people in his position are perfectly entitled to adopt. But the time for waiting is over, not least because the more often the controversy resurfaces, the wider the sore will open and the weaker will become the European challenge for the Belfry next year. He should declare firmly that James will be at his side next year. Either that or ask one of his closest friends to resign. He will certainly not embarrass him by any suggestion of dismissal.

Faldo will not go away. He is intent on exacting a mighty revenge on James for remarks in his book *Into the Bear Pit* which were perceived even by some of his supporters as disrespectful. You can well imagine how a voice in the team room at Brookline would have shouted 'Bin it!' when James held up a message of support from the unpopular Faldo. Torrance probably wishes now that James had decided not to reveal such a juvenile prank in his book. Much of the heat has been generated by that disdainful gesture and never mind that Faldo has behaved towards others in a similar fashion in the past . . .

But there is precious little else in the book for which James need reproach himself. So what if he has upset the American players, who seem slow to understand the damage they did to the game with their rampaging antics on the 17th green? So what if he suggested that Faldo would have to change his personality in order to ascend to the Ryder Cup captaincy? So what if he revealed that Colin Montgomerie had demanded David Feherty leave the team room at the hotel while under the impression that the Ulsterman, in his capacity as a television commentator in the States, had brought the 'Mrs Doubtfire' nickname to the attention of the American public? James, who praised the Scot and his wife Eimear warmly throughout the book, had checked with Monty if it was all right to include the story. He had no objection.

If Torrance were to canvass members of the team which lost to the Americans last October, he would discover a large majority – not far short of unanimity – supporting James in this matter. It could be that he will go down that road before issuing the kind of ringing endorsement which he obviously feels. James would not be James if he had not already offered his resignation as Ryder Cup vice-captain in order to ease any pressure on Torrance. Torrance would not be Torrance (and a good friend) if he had not already refused to accept it.

This issue should not be allowed to drag on any longer. If Faldo has genuine support, then let it be heard. And if Torrance has the backing of the majority of players and officials, as is widely believed to be the case, let them come forward and put their case.

Fraser's views echoed mine. During these weeks I was often at a loss to understand why there was such a lot of fuss about not a lot at all. It may have been a bit hurtful to reveal how I had binned Faldo's good-luck letter to the team, but I considered the anecdote relevant to the situation and an insight into people's views of him. I never said that he was undermining the team effort, just that it seemed that way. At that time we had had enough of him sticking his oar in. He had also attacked me verbally twice during the final counting week for Ryder Cup points, and had then had a go at our number one player. It was the last thing I needed at the time, and I'm sure Colin Montgomerie felt the same way when he read what Faldo had said about him. But even though the comments were unforgivable, I was not out to get anybody – just to set the record straight.

There was a lot of mud being hurled, and a lot of it was landing at my door. I thought it incredible hypocrisy that some were suggesting I was not fit to be vice-captain because of the book, yet there was nothing to prevent Faldo being on the team after the way he had behaved over the years. Those with a different agenda saw the serialisation of my book as a good weapon, and it was being used by them as a means to get me removed and have a continental vice-captain installed.

This bandwagon had been kick-started by Jean Van de Velde at the Belfry during the Benson & Hedges in the second week of May when he spoke out vociferously in favour of such a move. It was a notion I firmly disagreed with because a captain should be free to select whomever he wishes as an assistant. I would have been incensed had I been forced to appoint a continental just for the sake of it. In fact, I would have resigned if my hand had been forced, simple as that. Faldo was even claiming that I had lost the trust of the players which was something of a surprise. 'The trust for me and for an awful lot of players has gone out of the window,' he told the press. 'If Mark is part of the next Ryder Cup, it's going to create a volcano. Who knows what will happen when it erupts. If you're going to sit in that team room, you have to be motivated and prepared to say some pretty tough things, such as what you feel about your opponents. The thought that somebody might be thinking that whatever's expressed would be great for their next book would be just too dangerous. I think a lot of senior members of the European Tour Committee are very upset about it all. Tony Jacklin, Bernard Gallacher and Seve Ballesteros have all done books in the past with no problem. But now suddenly a guy has gone over the boundary lines of revealing what goes on in a team room.' What Faldo failed to realise was that everything I wrote about what happened in the team room was first of all cleared with the players referred to. No confidences were broken.

The situation quickly got messier and headed into deeper waters. Faldo secured the support of Seve Ballesteros, Bernhard Langer and Van de Velde, who were backing him behind the scenes and in the press, but I was not without my sympathisers, most revealingly the members of my Ryder Cup team. Unfortunately everything was getting highly divisive, a state of affairs exacerbated by Faldo's PR people, who were working overtime. For whatever reason, they seemed to want an unnecessary situation to run and run.

The chance to clear the air with Faldo was difficult to orchestrate because, firstly, it was thick with the mud being hurled from his direction, and secondly, he was spending most of his time playing in America. Our career paths didn't overlap until Loch Lomond immediately before the 2000 Open at St Andrews, and by then the whole situation had become about as ridiculous as it could get.

I was trying not to say very much, but people kept asking, and Nick was going on about how he had been insulted, insinuating that I had not told the truth. To my mind, implying I was a liar was in fact a lie in itself. There were no lies in the book. I really did not want to inflame the situation, but there was no shortage of people willing to fan the flames and I wasn't sure where progress could be made or how the matter could be brought to a conclusion. It certainly looked as if Faldo and his backers had embarked on a search-and-destroy mission, and there are no prizes for guessing who was the target. Faldo had taken everything very personally and had clicked his PR team into overdrive. Accusations were thrown at me left, right and centre, all of which was rather unpleasant, especially to be called a liar when it was far removed from the truth. The people who had been so quick to talk and lecture about breaches in the code of conduct went missing when the air got muddy, but to call somebody a liar without justification or proof is right up there at the top of the list.

Then other players with grievances against me started to get involved. I think one of the reasons for that stemmed from my profile having been raised through becoming Ryder Cup captain, and unintentionally falling out with a few people along the way. Jean Van de Velde embarked on what turned out to be a fifteen-month whingeing mission about not having played in Brookline until the last day. It was as tough for him as it had been for me having to make the decision, but that was what I was there for and all I was interested in was doing everything for the good of the team. Without doubt it's far from easy to be sidelined for two days, but Van de Velde appeared at the time to be taking it well. I certainly didn't get any negative vibes from him or through either of my vice-captains on his behalf. I was hoping he realised that sometimes a player has to do exactly what his captain wants him to do. I was completely mistaken.

To say that I felt he took it with a lack of grace following the event would be an understatement. He obviously did not like the fact that he had been left out and felt he should have played before the singles. He was so upset that I think he said at one point he would write to the Ryder Cup Committee to ask them to bring in a rule so that everyone played before the singles. I don't know if the Ryder Cup Committee discussed it, but it's obvious to me that the idea has no merit. A captain should have the ability to leave out members of his team until the singles – that is all part of that type of golf. It would be equally wrong to say that everyone should play every series. I think the current format of the Ryder Cup which has been around since 1979 – a series of four fourball matches and four foursomes matches on each of the first two days followed by twelve singles matches on the last day – works pretty well. I don't think there were many on Tour who supported Van de Velde's viewpoint whereas a number of people did question the value of the opinion of someone who had played in only one Ryder Cup and had won just the one tournament in Europe.

This may have been a bit harsh on Jean, who is an intelligent fellow and a valued member of the Tournament Committee, of which I am chairman, but I have had difficulty rationalising his stance. I think he was simply aggrieved at not having swung a club in competition for two days, then equally pained that when he had to he didn't do particularly well. Whatever his reasoning, he went on and on about it.

When Sam Torrance announced me as one of his vice-captains in the early summer of 2000, Jean kicked his campaign into overdrive. He began to claim that there shouldn't be any more British people involved, that there should be a greater European representation among the captaincy team. To be honest, most players in Europe think of us all as Europeans, not as either European or British, but Van de Velde obviously has a different view. And, of course, when *Into the Bear Pit* was published he got stuck into that as well. He was having a whale of a time, but the amazing thing is that throughout all of this he never once came up to me and said 'I don't think you should have left me out' or 'I don't think you should have written that in your book' or 'I don't think you should be one of Sam's Ryder Cup assistants'. He never voiced any of those points to me personally, he merely seemed to want to get the attention of the press, and in that he was certainly successful.

Van de Velde seemed to feel so strongly about having me removed as one of Sam Torrance's vice-captains that apparently he wrote to the Ryder Cup Committee asking for my resignation. I was told he was under the impression that I had said Nick Faldo would make a bad captain, but I think that shows that, like many other people, he had not actually read my book. I did not say that Nick would make a bad captain, I said I felt that if Nick wanted to be captain he should get to know the players better. I don't think that was an unreasonable comment. I would like to stress this point so that it is clear: I do not think Nick would make a bad captain. In fact, he has the potential to become an excellent captain. No captain is perfect, and my minor suggestion should in no way be representative of my overall opinion of Nick's ability to do the job well. Nick has a number of assets that would be invaluable to a Ryder Cup captain. He is single-minded, will take decisions that he thinks are right and stick by them regardless of the consequences, and he has more experience than almost anyone else in Ryder Cup history. The suggestion I made about getting to know the players better is an aspect I felt would be to Nick's advantage. He has played more often in Europe since my book came out, but I still don't think it's an unreasonable comment. It does seem, however, that Nick has been making strides in that area since the summer of 2000.

It is essentially the Ryder Cup Committee that appoints the captain, although generally the committee of the Tour puts forward a nomination, one which in recent years has been accepted. Following changes to the Ryder Cup Committee in future years this decision may well be taken by the Ryder Cup Committee alone, or in conjunction with the Tournament Committee. Either way, the man the players feel most comfortable with will be appointed, as in previous years. Whether Faldo will ever be named captain

I don't know. I think there are probably a couple of other players who might have claims on that position before him, certainly Woosy, Sam's vice-captain for the next Ryder Cup, and perhaps Bernhard Langer.

I have been asked if Jean Van de Velde went down in my estimation through his actions and words. To be honest, I think he went down in the estimation of a lot of people, not just mine. I was disappointed that he seemed to be trying to get under my skin because he was not far off succeeding, but he received relatively little sympathy from most Tour players, so I wasn't too worried. I would like to think that if I had a grievance with a player I would try to discuss it with him, and I definitely wanted to discuss the blow-up with Jean. Darren and Heather Clarke held a barbecue during the PGA at Wentworth and I approached Jean to assure him that if we were both involved at the next Ryder Cup I would simply be helping Sam and the team and would hold nothing against Jean himself. Jean said nothing of consequence and seemed quite happy, yet a day or two later he continued his whinge-a-thon. I think he simply wanted to have a go in the press, and when people decide to handle things in that manner it's a shame. He wanted people to hear him; not once did he ever come to me and say one word.

Van de Velde's attitude was in direct contrast to the two other players who, unfortunately, had also had to sit out the first four series. Andrew Coltart and Jarmo Sandelin behaved impeccably during the Ryder Cup and afterwards, and I'm sure any future captain knows that in those two he would have players who would fit into the team brilliantly. They are the kind of players captains would give their favourite sand wedge for.

The Frenchman's was not the only dissenting voice. Seve Ballesteros and Bernhard Langer also got involved, and they actually met with European Tour executive director Ken Schofield behind the scenes. Again, neither of them had read the book, although Bernhard, being a committee member, was urged to do so by Sam Torrance. It was a couple of months before he got round to it, at which time he immediately realised the error of his earlier criticism. Bernhard, although saying there were some things he would not have included, was good and big enough to apologise to the Tournament Committee for his earlier words. He said he would not have said what he did had he read the book initially. That was the reaction of a lot of people when they actually got round to opening its pages. It was nowhere near as bad as they expected. It was, in fact, a balanced account of all aspects of the Ryder Cup, and particularly my dealings with Nick Faldo.

It was interesting that Seve became involved. Perhaps it was because I had decided not to play for Great Britain & Ireland in his own tournament, the Seve Ballesteros Trophy, earlier that year. He had never so much as uttered a word about my captaincy, and when I saw him after Brookline he had just said 'hard luck'. When the Ballesteros Trophy was first put together in the January of 2000 we were told it would be held in April and the money would be low – guaranteed at no more than £10,000. Often I don't start playing until about that time of year anyway, and I'd already made plans for a holiday, so when I made the team I elected not to play. I know we play the Ryder Cup for nothing, but this was something completely different, and I knew I would probably be the weakest link not having played at all before it. It was no more than five weeks before the event was being staged that I received another fax saying things had changed and the money was now significantly better. I could have just turned up and taken it, but that would have been unfair. I just didn't want to go and play badly, which is what I suspected I would do.

I decided to stick to my earlier plans, and that obviously upset Seve because during the week of his tournament it was reported that he'd launched a tirade on different aspects of my Ryder Cup captaincy. I confronted him about his comments at the Spanish Open, but he claimed he had said none of them, that it was purely a fabrication by the press. I could only shake my head and walk away.

It seemed there were people who were looking for any reason to have a pop at me. I was accused of writing the book only for money, which is nonsense. Of course the money I earned from it was welcome, but be honest: how many authors out there write books for free? I wanted to write the book primarily to get what I felt down in print. I genuinely felt it would be worth writing, that it would be an entertaining read. By and large, although the true contents of the book were overshadowed by press articles, a lot of people have come up to me and said it was a really good read, which is exactly what it was intended to be.

The bandwagon continued to gain speed, Faldo going full steam ahead, his PR company shovelling coal into the furnace by the lorry load. I don't know if he was trying to gain credibility and improve his chances of being a future captain. It was conceivable, but he also claimed that the book was serialised to coincide with him being away, which was quite incredible considering he is usually away.

Anyway, I had nothing to do with the date of the serialisation – that was purely up to the *Daily Mail*. But I felt strongly that he was out to get me, and it emerged later that he had sent bottles of vintage port to those journalists who had supported him during the campaign against me. (I wonder how many of them sent their bottle back saying they were totally unbiased in their writing and could not accept such a gift?)

The press coverage in a way was ridiculous and far from objective. It was not a black-and-white situation, just a difference of opinion between two players, and neither of us should have been strung up the way we were. I felt Faldo had cast the first stone by criticising me during the build-up to the selection of the wild cards for Brookline in 1999, and I had responded the following year by putting into print what I and many other players felt. I had also included a couple of stories from the past about Nick and a bit of a summing up of his career in Europe. I felt it was perfectly balanced, but obviously that was not how it came across to him.

I was hoping that we could make some progress at the players' meeting at Loch Lomond the week before the 2000 Open, although I was again criticised in the press for being in the chair when the matter would be discussed. I hadn't really given my side of the story an awful lot, so I felt I had every right to be there. In any case, we have a very good committee full of strong-willed individuals, not frightened of asking pertinent questions or voicing their opinions. As Tournament Committee chairman it is my job to make sure that the committee as far as possible reflects the views of the membership. Although I may have an opinion – in this case coloured by events in 2000 – they are not necessarily relevant to the views of the member-ship. I had spoken about it to Ken Schofield, who of course knew the views of Faldo, Ballesteros, Langer and Van de Velde prior to the meeting, and, like several of the players, he asked me why I had written certain things in the book. I repeated to him that all those who had read it had felt it a reasonable and balanced account of events, they just hadn't been presented like that in the serialisa-tion.

The Tournament Committee meeting was a particularly lively one, the discussion about the book and its conse-quences long and frank. A couple of players voiced considerable reservations. They thought I was in the wrong and should not have gone ahead with the book, but they had only read the *Daily Mail*'s version. I could not stress enough that this was a completely different animal to the book, that it was not a hatchet job on Faldo. Those players in the room who had read *Into the Bear Pit* had a slightly different story to tell, and I also explained the similar feelings of the other players at the Ryder Cup when it came to Nick's behaviour. I think everybody began to see both sides of the story.

I finally managed to see Faldo on the bonny banks, but at that time things were seriously ugly. Our paths crossed just after the committee meeting which had given me its 100 per cent support and backed me to continue as Sam Torrance's vice-captain. I asked if he wanted to sit down and discuss the matter. He declined, saying he was concentrating on his golf and it was best to leave it until after the Open. I suspected he didn't want the matter resolved just then because he felt he could keep putting pressure on the Ryder Cup Committee, maintaining his attacks in the press and getting some kind of result. Ultimately, that is what happened.

The main worry of the Tournament Committee and staff was that the row was showing no signs of dying down – principally because Faldo kept insisting that I should resign as Ryder Cup vice-captain, from the committee and probably the board as well – and that the sponsors were starting to get uppity about the arguments overshadowing the tournament. I explained at length the details of the event that caused the row and told them I would be willing not to say another word about it, if it would help the situation. They accepted my explanation and gave Sam and his choice of deputies 100 per cent support. I respected my promised vow of silence – not that I had said much anyway – in a bid to defuse things, but Faldo continued to fan the flames, insinuating that I had not been truthful. He managed to build up a fair amount of public sympathy too, because the other side of the argument was not being put. He kept going and, as far as I was concerned, forced the Ryder Cup Committee into some form of action.

Matters came to a head at the Ryder Cup Committee meeting a couple of weeks after the Open. The committee is made up of three members from the European Tour board and three from the Professional Golfers' Association. Our representatives are Neil Coles, John O'Leary and Angel Gallardo, the latter never having played in the competition, the other two not for donkey's years. I have never been quite certain who represents the PGA because there are so many of them in jackets at Ryder Cup time it's difficult to determine exactly who is on the committee and who is not. But I do know that a lot of today's players consider all of them out of touch with the modern game;

certainly as far as the Tour's representatives are concerned there's a feeling that they're not representative of the players and should be replaced with younger blood. Apparently the committee did not discuss my book in any great detail and just wanted the whole thing to go away. They were determined not to be perturbed by arguments between players, but something had to be done.

I had spoken about the situation in detail with Sam Torrance, the first person to read the book. I had given him a copy before it was serialised and we had been in very close touch ever since. Neither of us saw any reason for the furore; if Sam did, he didn't tell me about it. Obviously, as captain he had to tread a slightly more careful line with the media, but we talked regularly, hoping the situation would resolve itself.

That was the way it was until that fateful Ryder Cup meeting, when it became clear that the writing was not now in the book, but on the wall. The only way the situation was going to go away was for the Ryder Cup Committee to get me to resign. To my mind, they were obviously too gutless to make any real decision on the issues Nick and I were arguing about – or, to be more precise at that point, what Nick was arguing about. They wanted me to resign, and I didn't see any point in refusing. Sam got on the phone to me, ducking and diving between the cars at Wentworth, the European Tour's base, trying to avoid the press until everything was sorted out. We decided that the only way forward was for me to step down. Fortunately I was away on holiday at the time and escaped any post-resignation inquests.

It is easy to argue that Sam could have been stronger, but not everyone is the same in this sort of situation and certainly I don't blame him for the way things turned out. I will go too far in defending the way I feel about things sometimes, but other people are not the same. I certainly bear no grudge against Sam, these things happen. It has not affected our relationship at all.

Knowing the people who had made the decision, nothing that happened particularly surprised me, but Jane was mystified and wrote to the Ryder Cup Committee asking for an explanation of their view that I should resign. She is still waiting for a reply, but she's not holding her breath. She wanted to know what their logic was, and I think the reason they didn't reply was there wasn't any. They obviously felt they didn't have anything sensible to say to her, or they would probably have given her the courtesy of a reply.

Incredibly, after the Ryder Cup Committee announced that I had resigned Faldo did not leave it at that. He started going on about wanting me removed as chairman of the Tournament Committee. Eventually, I think it was Neil Coles who said in print that Faldo had not been whiter than white and it was now time for him to shut up. I think Faldo then decided that that would indeed be the best course of action. He had persuaded a number of people to climb on board his ship, but continuing his attacks was likely to become counter-productive to his cause. I think he realised he had got all he was going to get out of the situation.

I felt that had I dug in over the issue of the resignation, matters would just have been made worse. They could always, I assumed, sack me anyway. I had had enough of the whole thing to be honest. It seemed outrageous to me that although this was not affecting my future particularly, it was affecting plans for the Ryder Cup. For me in Brookline it had been very, very important to have Sam and Ken Brown as assistants. I relied on the information I got from them and I knew I could trust their opinions and judgement implicitly. It made a big difference to my captaincy. Similarly, Sam wanted two people as vice-captains he felt the same about, but now he was being denied his wish. It was his plans that were being put in jeopardy, not mine.

The unfortunate thing about the Ryder Cup Committee as it then was, was that they did not take a decision on what was right or wrong, just on how to get a certain result. They felt the best way to defuse the situation quickly was to get me to resign. Had they said to me 'We think you were completely wrong to write what you did and we think you should resign because of that', I might have had more sympathy with their deliberations, but that was not the case. In fact, I don't think more than one or two of them had read the relevant sections of the book.

My August 2000 resignation was not the only consequence. Unknown to the Ryder Cup Committee, an enormous gap had been created between them and the Tour players, one that has forced changes in their constitution. It would probably have happened anyway, but the affair certainly helped to precipitate necessary change. It became blatantly obvious that the people who were representing the Tour on the Ryder Cup Committee were simply not reflecting the views of the players at that time. They were sitting there and not taking decisions on behalf of the players. They were being negligent of their duty.

Things will be different now. Instead of a three-three split between the Tour and the PGA, the Tour will probably have six representatives, the PGA two, and the European PGA two. Those representatives will be taking decisions for the players, and that seems totally fair. The European Tour representation should be in control because they are the people providing the players. One thing I don't expect them to change is the issue of payment for playing in the competition. No one I have heard of in the European camp wants to be paid. That was the stance before the 1999 Ryder Cup when the Americans were demanding payment, and I'm sure that's still the case. Indeed, I am convinced that every European player would actually pay to play in the Ryder Cup.

18. FACE TO FACE WITH FALDO

Under normal circumstances I take little interest in other players' tee-times, but things were different when I arrived at St-Nom-la-Bretêche on the outskirts of Versailles in the middle of September for the 2000 Lancôme Trophy, one of the oldest events on the European Tour calendar. I was particularly keen to discover when Nick Faldo was playing so that I could arrange to have what are generally known as 'clear-the-air talks'. How clear things would be by the end of it I was totally unsure, but it had to be done.

It was time to chat, particularly since quite a few people were asking when we were going to sit down together and sort out our differences. That had thus far proved tricky because Faldo was often out of the country – I don't think he'd been in Europe since the Open at St Andrews. At the Lancôme I discovered he wasn't far behind me in the playing order on the first day, so I decided to try to collar him after we had both finished our round. I asked tournament director John Paramor if there was anywhere we could meet in private and he suggested one of the Tour's mobile offices in the tented village.

I waited for Faldo to leave the eighteenth green and sign his card, then asked him if he wanted to sit down and have a chat. He looked a little surprised, but agreed, and we locked ourselves in the portakabin. I was eager to get everything settled because I'm not one to carry grudges, and I assumed Nick was the same.

We started by talking about the interview just before the Ryder Cup in which he had spoken at length about Colin

Montgomerie. I had been angered by what I had read for it seemed Faldo was trying to undermine our chances of winning in Brookline. The attack on Monty could not have come at a worse time. The Ryder Cup was less than a fortnight away and I had been doing everything I could to ensure complete unity, happiness and confidence within the squad. Faldo admitted that he had said Monty liked playing in his own backyard, but said that everything else after that had been made up by the press.

He also said that he had thought I didn't want him on the 1999 team because I hadn't given him any encouragement during the year, as Tony Jacklin used to when he was captain. Well, Tony never gave me any encouragement. I asked Sam Torrance if he had ever had any, and he said no. I think Tony must have encouraged Faldo because he recognised he was the type of person who needed it. I certainly didn't encourage many players, if any, during my captaincy. I didn't feel any of them would need an extra incentive to get into a Ryder Cup team. I always tried not to be too vocal in that respect with the players anyway, simply because it's easy to be misunderstood. In 1991, Bernard Gallacher discussed the make-up of the team before the event with Eamonn Darcy, who looked certain to be an automatic choice. Eamonn was under the impression that if he did not qualify automatically he would get a wild card. In fact, Eamonn missed the last counting event and was pipped for the last spot by David Gilford. He was off fishing somewhere when Gilly sneaked past him by no more than £200. Eamonn was expecting to be in the team, but he was mistaken, so I was always extremely wary in that respect not to say anything like 'you'll make it' or 'you're in'.

Then again, I had indeed spoken to Faldo early in the 1999 qualifying period, at the Benson & Hedges in Oxford in May. I told him that the press were asking about him and I had told them I wanted him on the team, but that he would have to show some form first. I know sometimes these statements can appear ambiguous, so I wanted Faldo to know exactly what the position was. I added that if he heard anything else then it would not have come from me. If that was not encouragement, what was it? He knew I wanted him on the team, but that I wouldn't have anyone on the team who was playing badly. By the time the last counting event, the BMW International, came along it was obvious Faldo was not playing well enough to get into the team. I told him that even if he had won that tournament in Germany it was doubtful I would have selected him because I was unlikely to go beyond position number twenty on the money list, and I would have had to go below that to find him. But Faldo was extremely critical of me at that time and it was upsetting.

I carefully explained to him why I felt so strongly about his comments about Monty, and why I, after consultation with others, including some players, had decided to put his good-luck message in the bin. 'Who were the other players in the room who agreed with you?' he asked. I wouldn't tell him; I thought that would be unfair. I said I did not feel I should drop anyone else in the muck. Obviously the binning of the good-luck letter was probably the one thing that made him more cross than anything, but I felt the episode illustrated how strong my and others' feelings were at the time.

I think Nick accepted that what I said was true, and I accepted that his words were uttered in good faith, although I didn't agree with them. Before we parted I asked him if he had read the book, and he said no, so I told him that he should because in my view the chapter in question was not as bad as the serialisation had made it appear. I had made a number of positive comments about him, and I felt that if he read the book he would at least see a balanced assessment of my dealings with him and my suggestion that an improvement in his relationships with other players would enhance his chances of election to a Ryder Cup captaincy. I think Nick has been at work in that respect, and I think he's probably keen to do the job – certainly more keen than he was a year or two ago.

It was probably a good thing that we got our grievances out in the open in what was a meeting that lasted about twenty minutes to half an hour. Tempers were fairly even throughout and there was no shouting, although it was obvious Nick was angry about certain things, but then so was I. I don't think we were ever going to agree on an awful lot, but we both had our say and I think we both said enough. We decided to tell the press that there were two sides to every argument and leave it at that.

Looking back, I have far more sympathy for Nick's point of view than those of the likes of Van de Velde and Seve who jumped on the bandwagon. I think now that Nick's grievances were honestly meant, even though whether or not they were justified is arguable. I think he partly got his way, and we both moved on. The next time we saw each other was when I made my comeback at the PGA at the end of May 2001 and I thanked him for the get-well card he sent during my fight against cancer. I think it was well intentioned; it was certainly received that way. When you become ill like that, everything is put into perspective.

Now we must wait to see if Faldo gets his wish to become a Ryder Cup captain. It will be very interesting, but for now that job is in the very capable hands of Sam Torrance, who for 2002 has a formidable opponent in Curtis Strange.

19. CAPTAINS COURAGEOUS

I first came across Curtis Strange at the 1975 Walker Cup, but I remember little of him other than the fact that he appeared to be an extremely dedicated golfer and slightly aloof – traits I was more than familiar with. It would be some time later that I started seeing more of him, although I don't think we played in the Ryder Cup against one another until 1989.

There can be no doubt that he has been an outstanding player and possesses an extremely good golfing brain. In his prime, he was as good as anybody – not particularly long, but a US Open type of player, which is easy to say now because his two majors were won at his country's national championship. But to win the season's second grand slam event a golfer has to be patient, precise and a good putter, and Curtis fitted comfortably into those categories.

I always respected him as a player and as a person, and without doubt he will be a formidable captain, not least because of his ability to communicate with the players. Listening to him now commentating on television, he comes across as intelligent and articulate, so if he wants something from a player or that player wants something from him, I think he will definitely be up to the task.

I know a captain's influence is not necessarily decisive, but when he had to pick his wild cards they appeared to be inspired choices. Both Scott Verplank and Paul Azinger went on to show extremely good form in the few weeks after their election, and in a way it would be extremely unlucky for Curtis if they were to show poor form in the run-up to the 2002 Ryder Cup. The decision to leave out Tom Lehman, who was eleventh on the money list and the first in line after the automatic selections, was an extremely brave one. I would have been more than tempted to select him. Indeed, I would go so far as to say he would have been in my team.

Lehman and I are not the best of buddies, but I would have found it tough to leave him out. He didn't agree with some of the points I made in *Into the Bear Pit*, although I stand by every word. Oddly, at the St Andrews Open in 2000 I was doing a book signing when his wife Melissa came forward holding six copies. I couldn't believe it, because it was obvious they had not been best pleased with what was in there. I think I signed one to George Bush, and heaven knows who else, and as I was signing them she started to bend my ear about the content. She got six signed books, I got an ear bashing.

The only time I have seen Tom since was at the Open in 2001. I failed to qualify, but went to Royal Lytham for the BBC. I was walking around the course before the championship started, having a look for commentary purposes, and he happened to be on the first tee when I got there. We exchanged pleasantries and then I walked away, believing it was in both our interests not to spend a lot of time together.

Tom and I may not be best mates, but I recognise the fact that he is a tremendously gifted player, extremely good under pressure. There aren't many people I'd pick over him to win a clutch match late on a Ryder Cup Sunday. A lot of players thought Curtis had left Tom out because of the crowds, that he thought Lehman's presence might provoke some anti-US crowd feeling at the Belfry. To be honest, I have no idea if this is true and without doubt Curtis would deny it even it were. Whatever the truth of the matter, Verplank and Azinger proved to be on form straight afterwards and more than justified their selection.

As a captain, you do sometimes get asked questions on certain issues over which you have to take a stance. If you take the wrong stance or give a wishy-washy answer and are seen not to be supporting one of your players in some way, then that can undermine the confidence in the team and the captain to some extent. But to be honest, you have to be somewhat naive to fall into the traps the press are likely to throw your way, although I'm sure they're forever working out ever more subtle ways of trying to trip up captains.

Overall, Curtis has handled the run-up extremely well. He said all the right things regarding the crowds in 1999, he said all the right things about Sam and about the way the team was shaping up, and from what I've seen he has proved he is certainly up to the job, with room to spare. It also looks as though he's enjoying it, throwing himself into it.

Curtis has been working in the media on TV for a few years now, and I think that's a big help when handling certain elements. As captain, you need to be fairly guarded about certain players and certain situations, but he has a knack of being guarded yet still saying something. If you're guarded and say nothing you start to appear as though you don't know your own mind. I think Curtis has pretty much got the balance spot-on. America will be a stronger team for having him as its leader.

Opposite number Sam Torrance has also taken to the job like a duck to water. He set his stall out early on by restricting his tournament appearances and doing more corporate work. He has certainly done an awful lot of personal appearances, company days and the like, and I think it has affected his golf, but he must have realised that was going to happen because when he got the job he signed up with Mark McCormack's International Management Group. In a way, having fewer commitments to tournaments has made it easier for him to concentrate on the Ryder Cup job. He certainly seems to have far more time to give interviews and talk to the media than I had. I played a full schedule as captain in 1999 and restricted private interviews to a couple a week. Sam, though, has kept himself relatively free to talk at length to many different people, which is obviously good for the press in general, and I think he has spoken well. Like Curtis, he is articulate enough to put his thoughts into words that are entertaining enough to get everyone listening, and that's important. It is always nice for the team to have a captain with a bit of personality. It was also a big help that he was at Brookline, so the comments he has made on that Ryder Cup come from first-hand experience. All in all he is managing the job extremely well.

Unlike Curtis, I don't think Sam had much of a choice with his wild cards. I have yet to talk to anybody able to put up even a half-reasonable case against the selection of Jesper Parnevik and Sergio Garcia. The only question mark came early in the season in the States when Jesper was out with a hip injury. Had he shown indifferent form when he came back his wild card might have been in doubt, but Jesper started to play solidly again and had a good Open, finishing in the top ten. He had other good tournaments too, and you know with Jesper that he can play under pressure and gels well with the other players. Although he partnered Sergio in the last Ryder Cup and Sergio also got a wild card, I think Sam can quite safely pick either one of them on their own to pair other people. Some would have liked Sergio to get in automatically to give Sam an extra option, but to be honest I think he has pretty much got the best team.

I know José María Olázabal was very disappointed to miss out, but he had every chance to make it. He won the French Open and moved, if not into the top twelve, then very, very close during the middle of May. He played in an awful lot of counting events after that but dropped down the list. Although you can rely on Olly to raise his game for the Ryder Cup, I don't think he had much of a case this time for a wild card. It was unfortunate that a prominent article appeared in the papers soon after the selection was announced in which Nick Faldo was quoted on why he thought Olly should have been picked. My guess is that Nick was fairly mortified when he saw the extent of the article because, rumour has it, he rang IMG the next day to send an apology Sam's way.

Had Sergio made the team automatically, there would have been an extra wild card going spare, and to my mind it would have been close between Paul Casey, Ian Poulter and Olly. It would have been a hard pick for Sam. I would have gone for either Poulter or Casey. Ian played extremely well for a long period of time and he has that touch of attitude I always think is an asset in Ryder Cup situations. Paul is obviously a huge talent and he too played some tremendous stuff. He literally played a handful of tournaments and forced his way close to the top twelve. On that type of form, he had to merit serious consideration.

All in all, given the same scenario that has faced Sam, I would have picked the same people, and my guess is that pretty much everyone Sam asked would have said the same. I think the twelve players Sam chose in 2001 were the strongest available; the big question is, what will happen come September 2002? Which of those players will be off form? It's going to be incredibly interesting because the worst situation any professional golfer can be in is to be under serious pressure and off form. That can happen prior to any Ryder Cup, but with the match being delayed a year, the chances of that happening are increased dramatically. It will be exactly the same for the Americans, though, and possibly worse, because they have an older team. When the Ryder Cup is finally played the chances of seeing knees knocking will be higher than normal because of the extra year.

Early in my career, I didn't feel pressure an awful lot. I don't know if that was down to my nature or the exuberance of youth, but the possibility or ramifications of failure simply passed me by. I think as you get older you suffer a little bit more in that respect. There was one occasion during a Ryder Cup match in 1989 when I stood over an important putt and couldn't move my legs, and several times during my 1995 singles win over Jeff Maggert I felt sick, but generally I have come through my career relatively unscathed in this respect. There's no doubt the one time I probably did feel most uncomfortable at a Ryder Cup was in 1993 when during the build-up I played very, very well and made the team easily, but by the time of the match I was really hopelessly off form. To be thrust into a pressure situation when you can't hit a cow's arse with a banjo is not nice to say the least. I felt the galleries were in danger on certain holes, but fortunately metal woods had come into the game by then. Had I been using a persimmon I think the Red Cross would have been involved.

Even though I've been removed as vice-captain for the forthcoming Ryder Cup, I have discussed all aspects of it fairly regularly with Sam. Generally, we seem to see things pretty much the same way. I think it's good for a captain to have people he can ring up and get an unbiased view from. I certainly used Sam and Ken Brown for that when I was captain.

20. TEAM TALK

UNITED STATES OF AMERICA

PAUL AZINGER

Another golfer who knows what it's like to be told he is suffering from lymphoma, the former US PGA champion has made a wonderful recovery and was a popular choice among the other team members when Curtis Strange selected him as a wild card. Played consistently well during the qualification period and continued in similar vein after making the team. It will be interesting to see if, a year down the line, he has carried his good form forward, but he will still be a valuable asset in the team room.

MARK CALCAVECCHIA

Had a great year in 2001, particularly early season. His form could definitely be in question approaching the Belfry, and I think Curtis will be watching him like a hawk and trying to get him to play like he did in the early part of 2001. He has not played Ryder Cup since 1991 and will be keen to exorcise the demons that have been with him since that shock game with Colin Montgomerie when he contrived to halve a match when four up with four to play. At least he has had a decade to get over it. He is the sort of player you think would feature more in fourballs than foursomes because he can be inconsistent, but when he's playing well and his putter is working there are few who can score lower. I've played with him a few times and he's great to watch, simply because he doesn't do things like other people. He's unconventional, free flowing, hits it hard, but can time the ball beautifully. In particular his putting has graduated to a claw-type method. It looks as if his right hand is only on the club because it is superglued there. I would not like to try that method under Ryder Cup pressure, but Calc has been using it for a year or two now. I guess he knows what he's doing. We will find out.

STEWART CINK

I don't know much about Cink's game other than what I've seen on television or from rare glimpses on the practice range, but he looks a very, very solid player. He seems to have a love affair with fairways and rarely misses them, and he also hits a lot of greens in regulation. It's the kind of game that wears a course down. He always seems unhurried and that is a precious quality, particularly in times of intense pressure – and believe me, there is no greater level of intensity than at a Ryder Cup. It's his first match so it's difficult to know how he will react, but he has been around a few years now so I think he'll be able to cope. If he can't, he'll soon be found out, such is the stage and the occasion.

DAVID DUVAL

The big breakthrough came in 2001 when he claimed his first major championship, and it's easy to see why many believe there will be plenty more. He's a marvellous player with an inscrutable temperament, wonderful rhythm and an impeccable sense of timing. He may not quite be up to Tiger Woods's length, but he's pretty close. He flights it very, very high and his short game is good. There really are no holes in his game; certainly if he played with Woods it would be a heck of a partnership, but of course if you put them together and they lost it would be a bitter blow for an American captain.

JIM FURYK

Without doubt the most interesting swing on the American team. It's difficult to see how it works at times, but work it does. He takes the club up and out on the backswing, then loops it back down inside. It's a strange way of getting there, but the important thing is that he repeats it over and over again. There's a great deal of movement at the top of the swing, but he's helped by having a wonderful rhythm. He is good under pressure, chips and putts well, and has been consistently good over the last few years. No reason to suspect that he will not be in reasonable nick at the Belfry.

SCOTT HOCH

There will definitely be a question mark over Hoch, despite the fact that he showed great form in 2001. He's probably edging towards the end of his career as a Ryder Cup player, so whether the extra year will do him any good remains to be seen. I don't think the Belfry will suit his game either because he's not as long as many on the team, but he does have the experience to get the best out of his game. He's an in-your-face player who will not be intimidated.

DAVIS LOVE III

Love has been in contention a huge number of times and is unlikely to be intimidated by the Ryder Cup atmosphere, as unique as it is. Indeed, he seems to relish the situation, and is probably one of America's top four players, along with Tiger Woods, David Duval and Phil Mickelson. Like the other three, he is exceptionally long and hits the ball very, very high. That kind of game should be suited pretty well to a long and damp Belfry in September. At that time of year, however, it can also be windy, and any advantage in length can quickly be wiped out by a few days of equinoctial low pressure.

PHIL MICKELSON

Without doubt one of the best players on the American team. It must be just as baffling to him as it is to the rest of the world of golf how he has managed to avoid winning a major championship. He has always been a long hitter, but he seems to be launching the ball miles these days. Length is not his only asset either: he's one of the world's best putters and is also the recognised master of the lob shot from just off the green. It's an easier shot in America because there's nearly always a bit of grass under the ball over there. Try it in certain places in Europe and you might watch it go 140 yards past the hole. Tom Lehman is the only American with whom he has played more than once in either foursomes or fourball, so he'll need a new partner this time.

HAL SUTTON

If you had to cast somebody in the role of gunslinger for the American team, Sutton would definitely catch the eye of the director, along with Calcavecchia. I was not impressed by the way he tried to whip up the crowd in his singles match against Darren Clarke at Brookline, but there's no doubt he's a gutsy performer. His form tailed off up to and immediately after the selection of the team so he's certainly a player who may benefit from an extra year. He's a top-class performer when he's on Tour, certainly someone who relishes the pressure of the Ryder Cup arena. He has a shorter, punchier swing than many modern players, but with forearms like my thighs he still hits the ball long distances and flights it well enough to tackle any course.

DAVID TOMS

Probably more than anyone else on the American team, Toms appears to play more in the old style. He's a little bit short of many of the top players off the tee, but he's a beautiful iron player and repeatedly appears to pepper the pin from 170 yards in. He showed when winning the 2001 US PGA Championship that he has the game and the composure for the big occasion. That's probably because he has a simple rhythm and uncomplicated technique. He's also a very good clutch putter – another quality that will serve him well when standing over a seven-footer for a half. His first major should have been no surprise to anybody because he played tremendously all season. He looks to be a real find for the American team, somebody who could partner just about anybody. When the selection process started he was not somebody I would have considered, but he has crept up on the blind side of world golf. Now he's there, he appears to be extremely comfortable lodged inside the upper echelon.

SCOTT VERPLANK

Scott seems to have been around for donkey's years, but that's probably because he was still an amateur when he won a PGA Tour title. He has always looked very solid from tee to green, and 2001 was a vintage year for him. He's definitely one player Curtis Strange will be hoping keeps that form for another year. I have never played with Scott so I don't know much about his game, but one thing is for certain: Curtis would not have picked him had he not been any good. He has had plenty of bad luck with injury, but has proved that when a suspect elbow is not giving him any problems he is a match for anybody, and a very gritty competitor as well.

TIGER WOODS

There's not much you can say about Tiger without using up all the superlatives in the dictionary. Put simply, he is that good, although last year he was perhaps not as good as in previous years. He's an extremely dangerous player, like Sergio Garcia on the European side capable of incredible things. He has not enjoyed huge success in Ryder Cups to date, but he's too good for that to continue for ever. Without question he will become a consistent points scorer.

EUROPE

THOMAS BJORN

He's the type of player every captain wants in his team, and I was very disappointed that he didn't make it in 1999 after impressing on his debut two years earlier when he was four down to Justin Leonard and came back to claim a half. He has matured into a tremendous player. He hits the ball a long way, and very high if necessary, putts well and aggressively, and is the sort of player who can take the course by the scruff of the neck and shake it into submission. He won't be frightened by anyone, and he's probably at his best when his back is to the wall. He just gets stuck in, and if he goes behind you feel he'll stage a comeback. In the context of the Ryder Cup, that can be invaluable. Eking out that extra half point can make all the difference come the end of the week.

DARREN CLARKE

The Ulsterman has become a superbly consistent player over the last few years and has done everything in the game except win a major and the Order of Merit. He has won one of the world championship events, claimed titles all over the place, and he seems to have become better and better. His game looks pretty much faultless. He hits it long and straight, he can do pretty much anything with his irons, and he's also a very good wind player. He played golf when he was young in windy places in Northern Ireland, and this is a skill he has taken into the professional ranks. Added to all these qualities is the fact that he's good under pressure, and therefore very likely to play all five rounds.

NICLAS FASTH

I don't know a great deal about Niclas's game, but what I do know is that his performance at the Open in 2001 was very, very impressive. He got up there and was obviously in with a chance of doing well fairly early on in the back nine, if not sooner, and he didn't buckle at all. He played extremely solidly right the way to the end in difficult conditions on a difficult course. His runner-up spot to David Duval obviously boosted his confidence because he continued to play well for the rest of the season. I suspect he is not a one-year wonder, and I think the Belfry will suit a long, high hitter like him.

PIERRE FULKE

Not enjoying the best of form at the time the Ryder Cup should have been played in September 2001, the Swede will probably benefit from the extra year to get back into shape and the kind of outstanding ball-striking we all know he is capable of. His play in the early part of that season showed he is obviously enormously talented and able to compete with the best. He will also relish the Ryder Cup situation having already proved just how good he is in match play in the one world championship event dedicated to that form of the game. Will relish the chance to get his teeth into a Ryder Cup.

SERGIO GARCIA

The young Spaniard is mercurial, to say the least. He's capable of extremely low scores and can do tournament-defining things. He has got that charismatic, sparky streak of a Ballesteros in him which enables him to hole chip shots at the right time, get an outrageously lucky bounce, and knock three woods to two feet just when you need him to. He just has that flash of inspiration about him, and you find that in very, very few players. Put a player like that into a team situation and he's worth his weight in gold. Just having him in the team room is like having a point on the board. He gelled tremendously with the team at Brookline and was good entertainment. Not that the team needs it, but he does bring vitality and energy, and to have that around is always good news for a captain.

PADRAIG HARRINGTON

The Dubliner seems to get better and better. He was second in the money list in 2001 and seems to clock up second places like they're going out of fashion, but I don't think it's his fault. You can get into runs like that, and I think eventually he will snap out of it in a big way and become more of a winner. He showed at the Volvo Masters that a player of his standard needs only the tiniest bit of luck to win, and I think in 2002 he will have more firsts than seconds. Tee to green he is rock solid, on the greens he is rock solid, mentally he is rock solid. He started to show these valuable qualities at Brookline, and he has gone from strength to strength since then. I would be very surprised if he weren't on form at the Belfry.

BERNHARD LANGER

I know how upset Bernhard was not to be playing in 1999, and he effected something of a renaissance in his form in 2001. In fact, I don't think he has ever looked better from tee to green, and his driving has improved enormously. He finished close to the top twenty in the American money list and was top ten in Europe, and to do that on both Tours is evidence of an incredible standard of golf these days. He may find five rounds tough, but we have plenty of young, strong players who can easily play five, so I would probably look for Bernhard to play three matches out of the five, if not four. A lot will depend on his form in the 2002 season, but from the way he was swinging in 2001 – better and more balanced than I have ever seen it – I would pencil him in for another good year. His short game is just fantastic, and that's probably the most decisive part of the entire package. A lot is said about his putting, but even when he was occasionally suspect and using the short stick he was topping putting statistics regularly, and now he is no longer subject to the odd yip. He has closed up what minuscule holes there were in his short game, and that takes the pressure off your long game.

PAUL MCGINLEY

Had nothing short of a tremendous year in 2001 when he played far, far better than ever before. He has found length off the tee, and I think that kick-started his game to some extent. Working with Pete Cowen, he seems absolutely comfortable technically. I don't know how much Pete says to him, but it doesn't look like a huge amount. He just seems to tweak Paul's game every now and then, then tells him to go out and play well, which he invariably does. I followed Paul for one round at the 2001 Benson & Hedges at the Belfry. I was out on the course working for the BBC, and he barely hit a bad shot for eighteen holes. He was tremendously impressive, and I think he finished second that week. That bolted him right up into Ryder Cup contention, but he continued playing like that pretty much the whole season. He really does deserve his Ryder Cup berth because his game has moved up a level. He has gone from being a good player who would win the occasional tournament to being a Ryder Cup player who has the capability of winning three or four tournaments a year. It's not easy to move up a level like that, and it has taken a lot of hard work, but Paul's not afraid of that and will be keen to clock up a few points as quickly as possible in September. Although a Ryder Cup rookie, he has the maturity and experience to cope with the pressures of the big occasion.

COLIN MONTGOMERIE

Monty was magnificent in Brookline. His game has gone off a wee bit since then and he has stopped winning money lists, but he is still a tremendously good player who finished high in the Order of Merit in 2001 – a feat he seems to pull off without breaking into much of a sweat. I get the feeling he has got more money list titles in him, and I think he's another player who may benefit from the twelve-month delay. He could just be firing on all cylinders come September, as long as he has recovered from his back problems, because the Ryder Cup does seem to bring the best out of him. His performance under pressure at Brookline was remarkable given the circum-stances and the hostile atmosphere. Colin is someone the players look to as their sort of number one performer – a player who is bound to make a few points for the team. The others know they just have to help him and they've got a good chance of doing the job.

JESPER PARNEVIK

The American-based Swede was out with an injury for part of 2001, but he finished the season playing very solidly. His swing doesn't seem to have changed at all over the years, and he looks totally comfortable with his method and technique. Although slightly steeper than textbook, he is certainly pure through impact. He was great at Brookline in 1999 and will be someone Sam Torrance can rely on at the Belfry. I don't think any of the Americans will particularly relish the prospect of facing him in tandem with Sergio Garcia again.

PHILLIP PRICE

The Welshman was the surprise package of the Europe team. He was not someone you would have picked two years ago, but I don't think anyone has improved as much as he has over the decade he has been on Tour. When he first emerged he was short off the tee, not a great iron player and relied mainly on his short game to make an impression. He has chipped away at his long game year after year, and now he really is a very solid player. He has put on a lot of length and is probably one player who has been helped by technology more than others, but he still has the short game he had in his early days on Tour. He could go very well at the Belfry, and I think he might be worth a few bucks to win his singles.

LEE WESTWOOD

The Englishman is another player who will benefit from a year's delay. He had a rotten 2001 by his standards, mainly because he was so good in 2000 when he won the money list. He moved house, then he and his Scottish wife Laurae had a baby early in the year. Lifestyle changes can affect your game, but to be honest, later in the season he hadn't really shown much sign of a recovery. I think having the winter off just to work on his game and coming out fresh for the new season will see him back to normal. By the time of the Ryder Cup he should have worked his game back up to where it was and be one of the team's strongest players.

21. 11 SEPTEMBER

It had been an eventful two-year captaincy for Sam Torrance, and as September dawned the hard part in a way was over. He had watched carefully through the best part of a couple of seasons, checking player performance and trying to get all of the many and varied details, from uniforms to course preparation, right for the Ryder Cup. He had chosen his wild cards, which is always a worry (though Sam's choices hadn't been quite as difficult as mine in 1999). Just about all that was left to think about was the make-up of the pairings and how best to get the players practising in the run-up to the start of the match. Essentially, though, everything was done, dusted and ready to go.

And then came 11 September, or '9.11' as the Americans call it, although that did take a bit of getting used to because 9.11 in Britain is 9 November or eleven minutes past nine. No matter whether you put the day or the month first, the date 11 September 2001 will remain the day when all our lives changed. In much the same way that everybody remembers where they were when Elvis died and John F. Kennedy was shot, time will not dull the memory about what we were doing when disaster struck downtown New York and thousands of people lost their lives.

I was in Ilkley and couldn't get to a television, but I was listening to it on the radio and it was numbing to say the least. Apart from the shocking loss of lives and the devastation caused by the terrorists, it was immediately obvious that all sorts of things were going to be thrown into turmoil. The repercussions would ripple right across the board, affecting everybody's lives in one way or another. All airports in America were shut, the financial market crumbled, and we all waited nervously to see what the superpowers were going to do about one Saudi dissident.

Golf was among the first sports to be affected with the cancellation of the World Golf Championship event in Akron, Ohio. Everyone was stuck there for about five days. It was a good week or two, however, before they announced the postponement of the Ryder Cup for a year. To the authorities' credit they didn't jump into the decision, but I think everyone felt from the outset that the Americans would not travel. Historically, they tend to stay at home given any sort of trouble on a global scale, let alone something of this magnitude in their own back yard. I think the Europeans were ready to play after a few days' reflection. Many thought it would have been nice to play in a way that was slightly less intense and more in the spirit Samuel Ryder would have wished the matches to be played in. After what happened at Brookline I think that may have happened anyway, but perhaps 11 September was too close to the scheduled opening of the match. I think the bottom line was that some American players understandably refused to travel to Britain, so the decision to postpone was taken.

I think it was the best and the right decision, but something of a paradox, because I cannot see Americans being any safer in 2002 than they would have been in 2001. There was also something of a contradiction in what some of the American players were saying. They said it wasn't right to play it so soon after the Twin Towers disaster, but baseball carried on in America the following Monday. I think it was probably the prospect of international travel that was the real worry for them. We have had far more experience of terrorism because of the IRA – largely financed, ironically, by American dollars.

I never thought there would be any show of hostility in the matches this time round. I think the only time there will be any, if ever, is when it's played in America and the home side is losing. European crowds just don't react in the way American crowds did in 1999 if their team is losing. It will be a very sad day for golf if I am proved wrong. Ryder Cup crowds have been very good on both sides of the Atlantic, with the exception of Brookline and the slighter exception of Kiawah Island in 1991 when there was obviously some trouble, although personally I didn't experience any.

Still, there could be little argument over the decision to postpone the match. It gave captains Torrance and Strange another year to assess their teams, and I can't help but think that because the American team is older than ours they have more chance of being affected by the postponement than the Europeans.

There seems little doubt that several of the pairings that would probably have started at the Belfry in 2001 will still be matched up in 2002. Some of them will have endured from the Brookline encounter.

Jesper Parnevik and Sergio Garcia were extremely happy together in 1999 and I think everyone would expect them to be paired again, certainly at the start of the week. Lee Westwood and Darren Clarke played comfortably together too, so there's every chance they'll start together, although

241

hopefully Westwood will be playing a damn sight better than he did in the build-up to the postponed match.

Colin Montgomerie, the rock of the European team for the last few matches, will need a new foursomes and fourballs partner, for fellow Scot Paul Lawrie, who performed admirably on his debut, did not make the team this time. It has happened before to Monty, because having won two out of three matches with Bernhard Langer in 1997 the German failed to make my team, although he came very close to getting a wild card. That is a partnership that could be resurrected, but a lot depends on how many rounds Langer will be playing during the week. I think if Monty is playing at all reasonably, he will want to play five times. He's a big strong chap who doesn't appear to get tired, at least he certainly hasn't to date.

If Colin's playing well and his creaking back is no longer groaning, Sam will be keen to play him in five, but you never know when the captain might think it better to rest him at some stage. He will be looking for clues from all the players as to how tired they are to ascertain whether or not they're capable of playing five rounds, just as I did in 1999. The Belfry is a flat course, but it's long, and Ryder Cup week can be tiring. A lot depends on the physical state you're in and on how naturally strong you are in managing to stay on your feet for the length of time required. And of course there's the mental side of it. That can get wearing too. Some people feel tired after one round, others can go five without batting an eyelid. Sam will be talking to the players and their caddies and looking for clues from the vice-captain and assistants he has out on the course.

Thomas Bjorn has returned to the side after making such a positive impression in 1997 before struggling with illness and injury in the run-up to qualification for the match in Boston. I was very keen to have Thomas in the team of 1999, but he just happened to have one really bad year and he was nowhere near getting in, simple as that. He's a tremendously strong player who hits the ball a long way. He's the type who relishes match play as well. He will definitely be playing a lot, and whoever he partners it will be a strong pairing.

I'm not sure whom Thomas would prefer to play with. You could put him with Monty quite easily and that would be a fierce pairing, but there are plenty of permutations. Ten to twenty years ago players would say 'I don't want this, I don't want to play with him', but I think over the past few years things have changed. Now a player will know that if his captain wants him to play with someone else then he has to shift his arse, go out there and not complain about it. The players are all a bit more flexible nowadays, and they play with different people in practice as well to prepare them for that. I shuffled them up a lot in the build-up to Brookline just so that they knew they might be playing with different people, and I think Sam will do the same. There's definitely an element of 'if this doesn't work we'll try something else' during the Ryder Cup. Take Clarke and Westwood. If they lost even though they felt they were playing well, you could split them up and maybe make two good pairings. The bottom line is that both players and captain have to be flexible. If something isn't working you know as captain that you have to change it, and change it quickly, and the players will have to respond to the captain's wishes in that regard.

I expect Padraig Harrington and Paul McGinley to be a partnership. They played together in 1997 when Ireland won the World Cup, and my guess is that they will be keen to carry on where they left off. The two Swedes, Pierre Fulke and Niclas Fasth, are both Ryder Cup rookies, so I don't think they'll be paired together early on, and the same goes for Phillip Price. It would be preferable to filter them in, as it were, with more experienced players. A rookie pairing is always dangerous. You're not only liable to lose the match, you're liable to knock confidences, and that's something you don't want to do as it restricts your choices later on. There's nothing worse than getting out there that first morning, losing heavily and being worried about being put back in.

Ideally, you would want all twelve playing on the first two days and no one playing too much, but the sole object of the week is to get 14½ points and you have to send the players out in such a way as to achieve that. If that means not playing a player until the singles, I'm sure Sam will do that. There's no question that he would want all the players to have at least one match before the singles, but not at the expense of points. If that happened, I don't think your team would forgive you.

The Europe team is a younger one than the American side, but it's not all that short of experience and we don't have an inordinate number of rookies. They may be young, but they're a strong bunch, so Sam will have plenty of options.

Historically, the Americans switch around players a bit more, and captains nearly always play all their members before the singles, although I think it may well be a bit different this time because of the extra year's wait. More players on both sides could be off form so it may be that Curtis Strange won't be able to avoid leaving anyone out until the singles, but he may have a very difficult decision to make as to whether or not to do that.

What he does have are four players who are noticeably better than the others. Woods, Duval, Mickelson and Love were the highest in the world rankings when the American side was finalised. Play them together and they could make tremendously strong pairings; split them up and they lose, the damage to the team psyche could be immense. It's a tough decision to make, but there's no doubt that Curtis knows what he's doing. He'll know who's likely to fit with whom. He would have picked Paul Azinger and Scott Verplank because he felt they could play with anyone else.

Because of the years some of the Americans are carrying – they have five players around the 40 mark or older – Curtis may want to play few of them five times for fear of too many getting tired, so I suspect there will be a good deal of swapping and changing. But he too has a flexible side, so from that point of view I don't think Curtis will be too restricted.

It's difficult to see how Curtis sees Tiger Woods fitting in, and with whom. Does he put him with another top player to make his strongest pairing and risk wasting two aces in one hand? I think he'll look for someone other than Duval, Mickelson and Love as a partner for Woods, perhaps one of the younger players such as David Toms. He may actually integrate very well with Tiger, his accuracy blending with Tiger's power.

But of course all this is pure speculation. Both captains may well surprise us all at the Belfry in September.

22. THE BELFRY

It was difficult to see where a good course was going to come from when the Belfry opened in the 1970s. As fields go, it was a particularly big one, and hard underfoot. When it was wet it was messy, when it was dry it was too bouncy, and rarely were conditions a happy medium of those particularly unsatisfactory traits.

I think the problem stemmed from the fact that the course was built on pretty much a shoestring budget, and anyone who designs courses knows that if you don't have a great deal of money at your disposal you're not going to build a Wentworth. Still, the old Belfry had a number of good holes. I was on the border of liking it because there always seemed to be a bale-out side. I have always preferred that off the tee because it gives me a bit of confidence – my not being, in my opinion, a great driver. I tend to drive it better on courses that are not quite as tight. The Belfry always had the potential to become one of our finest, but in the early days it was never a particularly popular Tour stop. It is now.

A lot of money has been spent on the Belfry in the last few years. The re-design was done by former Ryder Cup player Dave Thomas, who really has upgraded it into a championship course of distinction. The trees that were planted have over the years grown to a good size. They have put in more new trees and lakes and switched a few holes around, and now there are no weaknesses. You have to hit the ball up the middle with the middle of the club, so it's no longer a course that suits my game, but its variety is impressive and, apart from maybe two or three holes on the back nine, it's pretty relentless. There aren't too many birdie opportunities, and although the three par fives are now all within reach under normal conditions, they are definitely no giveaways, so I can't see the 2002 Ryder Cup being a birdiefest. But if the greens are holding, and they should be in September, and the fairways are of a nice soft consistency, it should be an excellent test for players of world-class calibre.

The Belfry has been an ideal venue for the Ryder Cup over the years because there's a good hotel with plenty of rooms, the practice grounds are right there, and there's plenty of space for spectators on the course and for the corporate paraphernalia that accompanies events of this size.

HOLE 1

I played the Ryder Cup at the Belfry in 1989 and 1993 and the first was always not too bad. You could take a one-iron off the tee and chase it along up the right, just short of the right trap. It made for a gentle start, but now it will be a three-wood or driver because the course is a lot softer, particularly so in September, unless there's an unusually dry spell. Only the very, very long hitters would consider hitting an iron off the tee. It's imperative to miss the bunkers on either side of the fairway because the faces on them have been raised a little over the years. You really do need to be on the fairway here, and it's a far more taxing tee shot than in years gone by.

The perfectly executed drive – and don't forget that this is the Ryder Cup, when the sound of knees knocking can be heard above the sound of the M42 – will leave a mid-to short iron into the green. But it's difficult to say what clubs players will be using for their second shots because there's such variance in terms of the distances people hit. If you look at the shorter hitters in comparison to David Duval you're talking maybe 40 yards and four clubs. So the difference could be from a five-iron to a nine-iron.

The target's not such a huge one compared to some of the greens, but there are no great intricacies if you do find it. The ball always used to run off the back fairly easily, but at the Ryder Cup in September I think they will keep the greens relatively soft. Making the greens too hard would play into the hands of the Americans, because they hit the ball much higher.

HOLE 2
It's no longer as short as it was because a fairly insignificant hole has been turned into something more complicated, one that, like all the others now, commands respect. As par fours go, however, it's still not one of the longest holes, and I would think most players will take a long iron or three-wood to keep the ball in play and away from the sand and the other trouble. If the players have settled down and their knees aren't doing passable impersonations of castanets, when they stand on the tee they'll probably be thinking 'birdie chance', particularly if they find the short grass with their opening shot. If the tee shot is in good shape then it's a relatively straightforward mid- to deep iron into the green.

HOLE 3
It used to be a long par four and a very, very boring hole, but now it has been turned into a par five and one of the

best on the course – the main feature being the second shot over water for those long enough to consider going for the green in two. The biggest problem during Ryder Cup week will be the right-hand bunker, because that's about 290 yards to carry. I would expect the rough to have been grown in over that bunker to deter the long hitters from just flashing the ball over the trap and leaving a mid-iron into the green, and I would imagine that captain Sam Torrance will be narrowing the fairway there, otherwise the long/high hitters will have too much of an advantage. Generally it will be a drive between the bunkers and then a long iron, a lofted wood to a green that is difficult to hold.

The biggest problem with the third is that, being a new hole, you have to lay up to part of the fairway where the turf is not very well developed. You get quite a flat lie, but if it's dry it's tight, and if it's wet it's a bit muddy. Hopefully, that will have improved by September. If it hasn't, it will be quite easy to flop the ball into the water from there.

HOLE 4

This is not a tough hole, it's desperately tough, and a wonderful test of the golfing brain. It has changed with the third in that it used to be a par five and is now a four, and heaven help the golfer who doesn't play two great shots on it. It's unrecognisable from what it used to be like, and has been developed into one of the course's finest.

The best tee shot will be one that carries the bunker on the right. Club golfers will be interested to know that to carry that particular trap the ball has to travel a distance of 260 yards through the air – a journey most of the players will believe they can force their ball to make, but one which can be intimidating, particularly if the wind is against. Those who can get it over will be rewarded by the wider part of the fairway and a mid-iron to the green over water, which in itself is not a tension-free shot. The problems really arise if you can't carry that bunker, for the alternative is not an attractive one – downright ugly, in fact: you end up hitting the ball towards the left-hand trap up the fairway and it's only 280 yards to reach it. Your line is determined by the fact that the hole has an S-bend effect because of the strategic placement of the bunkers.

If you don't get right up to the bunker, don't hit it flush off the tee or hang back a bit too much to avoid it, you're going to have to go in with an awful lot of club, over water, to a green that's not huge considering the difficulty of the hole. I suspect there will be more bogeys than birdies here. The fact that the green slopes back to front does help you hold it, but even so, you've got to be fairly precise because you're trying to get it over the water. It wouldn't surprise me if Sam put the tee up a few yards on this one. If it's playing too long, it might give the long/high hitters too much of an edge.

That, of course, raises the question of whether a home captain should be allowed to tinker with a course to try to gain an advantage for his team. I have no qualms whatsoever in saying that how the course is set up is entirely the home captain's prerogative and an intricate part of the match, probably more so now when the matches are tight than in, say, the 1970s and early 1980s when the result was rarely disputed. Today, it would be silly for a captain to forgo any slight advantage he may be able to obtain from setting the course up.

When I was helping Seve in 1997 at Valderrama together with Miguel Angel Jiménez and Tommy Horton, the four of us spent a long time on the seventeenth hole discussing whether to leave the green hard so that no one could hold it with their second shot to the par five, or make it really soft so that everyone could hold it. The danger was that if you left it slightly holding, the Americans, who hit their long irons very, very high, would be able to hold it, whereas most of our guys wouldn't. As it turned out, about three inches of rain fell overnight so the decision was taken out of our hands.

HOLE 5
This is a simple but very good hole that makes very effective use of green shape. Players will reach for either a driver ·or three-wood, depending on the elements. You could hit a three-wood short of the right-hand trap, but if there's any wind it'll probably be a driver. There is water down the left, but not at a distance likely to influence either tee or approach shot.

The main feature of the hole is the green, which is a short and wide one, and players will probably be going in with a middle to deep iron. It's important to ensure that you get the distance and the flight right, to get the ball near the pin. When you get on to the green, it's relatively flat on the left and slopes down to a flat section on the right. The sloping section in the middle is too steep for a pin position, so essentially you have two smallish sections of green, top left and lower right. It's one of my favourite holes, one that proves they don't have to be extremely long to be tricky.

HOLE 6
This is another hole that has never really had much done to it, probably because it's difficult to know what you could do to it to make it any better. What hits you first as you stand on the tee is just how difficult the shot is going to be, the kind you have nightmares about. There's water left and it's quite firm on that side of the fairway, so the ball will tend to run off into the water. On the right there's sand and trees, so if you hit a driver or three-wood you want to be absolutely certain you know what you're doing. I think a lot of players will go for a long iron to keep it in play, which would leave a long to mid-iron to the green which again has water on the left, but not tight to it. The hazard is just about far enough away for you not to feel too intimidated. The big bunker on the right will probably catch more people. It seems regularly to attract balls and is a very good guard for a green that's relatively flat and quite large.

HOLE 7
This really is a very good hole. The first of the par threes has been changed significantly over the years and now plays somewhere between a four- and seven-iron, depending on pin position on a fairly long and narrow green. It used to have railway sleepers around the front, but I assume they got rid of them in case someone did themselves some damage and decided to sue the course for millions. Usually the wind is across, and that always makes a narrow green harder to hit. Par is always acceptable on this hole.

HOLE 8
A long, strong par four and a hole that wasn't changed too much in the re-design. There are a few more dangers down

the right, though, where a couple of bunkers are slap-bang in play for a driver. Right of those are trees, and there's water on the left – all in all fraught with problems for all those straying from the straight and narrow. The fairway has softened over the years because it used to be quite firm. The ball used to chase up left into the water with alarming ease, but now the fairway will hold the ball a bit more.

The perfect drive will leave a long or mid-iron into a reasonably sized green semi-protected by a ditch at the front, but far enough away from the green not to cause too many problems. The bunker on the left is a bit sunken, so that is probably the greater hazard. Although it's a decent enough size for a target, if you're going in with a lot of club it's not easy to hit. Again, this is just one of many good, tough holes on the course that was originally a Peter Alliss/Dave Thomas design.

HOLE 9

Another good par four that has had the bunker changed a little bit up the left. It used to be one huge flat bunker, but now has a bit of a lip on it. A lot may depend on conditions during the week and how the hole is playing, but Sam may choose either to push the tee forward or grow the rough over the back of that trap so that it's not too easy to set up a deep iron to the green. The green is over water and is further protected by a horrible bunker that's probably more of a hazard than the water. If you get in the wrong place in that bunker, its vertical face means it's virtually unplayable. The green is in three awkward tiers so it's tough to putt on. You rarely get a straight one, and judgement of pace is difficult.

If the hole is playing long, it's a very tough test. I think it may be better from a European point of view to push the tee forward and just play it with a driver and deep iron, but that's something Sam is going to have to decide during the week. It will depend on how wet the course is and also how far the players are hitting it. Some players can become much longer year on year if they change clubs or just start hitting the ball a different shape.

HOLE 10

Number ten has become one of the celebrity holes in golf, one all the spectators will want to have a good look at. Off the back tee, few players would ever go for the green, but if placed further forward it becomes a challenge to be carefully considered. Off the back, the carry to the front must be a good 260 yards, but if the tee's put forward it would only be about 210 to the front. At the Benson & Hedges for the last few years they've put the tee well forward on at least one day, and you can even get to the back of the green with a three-wood from there. The problem is that the green is a narrow target and under pressure it's easy to bail out and hit it straight right. Although it looks a bail-out, you would either be left with an impossible pitch over the humps and down and across the narrow green into the water, or you can actually hit the trees and come back into the water. So there's a lot of danger involved in going for it, but if you hit the required fade there's every chance you'll make a birdie.

I think for the Ryder Cup they may well pop the tee forward to some degree, but that just depends on how Sam sees the hole. It's a great hole for fourball matches because you can both take a whack at it or one of you can play safe and the other can have a go. To go for it in foursomes the tee would have to be very well forward, I think. If the tee is at all towards the back I just can't see people going for it, even in singles, unless they're four or five down.

If you lay up, it's a seven-iron off the tee, a wedge in and relatively simple, unless you get careless with the tee shot. If you start laying up too far to the left, you come in at an odd angle, particularly to a back pin, but if you do find the right place on the fairway you have a straightforward wedge, although if the green is very soft it's just about possible to screw it back into the water.

However it's approached, it's a great hole for spectators, who can see the entire hole from start to finish. That provides for good entertainment, especially for people who like nothing better than to see balls going in water, for whom it's an ideal place to sit. I have a few mates like that.

HOLE 11

The eleventh has been toughened up on both sides with bunkers, and a new one about 300 yards off the tee down the right has been designed by Sam Torrance. This one will catch those who have flown the existing ones at 260/270 yards, keeping the pressure on the big hitters and giving them a bit more to think about. For normal hitters it's a question of getting it between the bunkers and on to a fairway that's not too tight. There are few complications with an inviting green that slopes from back to front, and it's a relatively big target. If you drive sensibly the reward could well be a birdie.

HOLE 12

The re-design of this outstanding par three is probably the most complete on the back nine, if not the entire course.

It used to be a long slog to a sloping green with very few endearing features; now it has been shortened and incorporates a waterfall down the right. The general tightening up has made for a very good short hole indeed. Instead of a three-wood, you'll now have to go in with something between a three- and a five-iron depending on whether the pin is on the top or bottom tier. Although some of the difficulty has been taken out of the hole with the loss of yardage, it's still tough enough to drop a shot on very easily. It's essential to get on the correct tier with your tee shot because there's a very severe slope in the green. Anybody not on the right level could easily be staring at a three-putt. It's not too difficult a hole when the pin is on the bottom tier, though, because the slope can be used as a back stop, but the extra birdies you'll see there will be taken away when the flag flutters on the top level. Congratulations to designer Thomas here particularly because it's not often nowadays that holes are changed and made shorter, but this one is 100 per cent better for it.

HOLE 13
If the previous hole has been changed almost out of recognition, this one is very much as it has always been. It's a fairly uncomplicated and relatively easy hole when compared with many of the other par fours. An accurate drive to a generous fairway leaves little more than a wedge to a not overly tight green. The only danger really is the bunker on the right, but you really do have to hit a poor drive to find it. There's out of bounds to the left, but it's not tight to the fairway and I doubt anybody will be forced to reload off this tee. The toughest position will be to the very back of the green where it narrows, but if the flag is almost anywhere on the front half it should be birdie time.

HOLE 14

The bunker has been enlarged on this one, but other than that it's very much as Peter Alliss and Dave Thomas originally designed it. It ranges from a four- to a seven-iron, depending on the wind. It's a good, solid short hole with no real trouble, and the green is big enough to allow a player to aim straight at the pin and not be too worried about the consequences of missing the target.

HOLE 15

This is a solid long hole, reachable unless it's into the wind. If there's anything more than a gentle breeze, it does affect the thinking because you have to lay up either short of the green or short of the cross bunkers that are 50 yards further back. But if the conditions are right there's no huge penalty if you go for it and miss, although a three-tier green does make any bunker shot that bit more difficult. There's a ditch across the fairway, about 360 yards off the tee, but although the fairway slopes down to it, it would have to be an unusually big hit to reach it. The water is bordered by a few yards of rough anyway, so it's not really a factor unless you're a weekend golfer, in which case it may give you a problem on your second shot. If it causes problems during Ryder Cup week then either conditions are pretty difficult or some players are not on top form. It's a good hole because it does offer a chance, but there's trouble to be found, particularly off the tee. There are plenty of bunkers in the way of wayward tee and approach shots, so it's not impossible to get into a fair amount of bother. Even so, it's still definitely a birdie chance.

HOLE 16

Not that short, and quite tough now that it has been strengthened over the years by trees maturing and others being planted. It has become a good hole thanks to the tightening, and the bunkers have more of a lip than they used to. The fairway is a decent width now, and once you've got it on there the main problem is when the pin is on the right. The target area is very small on this higher tier and it does slope down sharply to the left. Find the bottom level with your approach and you're faced with a very tough putt. The upper level is almost like an upturned saucer. If you're going in with more than a seven-iron at the white-knuckle stage of a Ryder Cup match, it'll be quite a difficult shot.

HOLE 17

This is the last of the three par fives and one which has seen a fair amount of drama over the years, but mostly on the green, or near the end of the hole anyway. I would imagine Sam will be narrowing this fairway down as you go around the corner of the dogleg. The way it's set up normally, the longer you are off the tee the easier the hole is. Sam will not want that for Ryder Cup week, so we may see the rough being grown in at around the 300- to 320-yard mark. Once you've got it over the corner, depending on how much you have cut off, you're left with either a lay-up or a very long second, but the green is a small target and there are bunkers around 20 to 30 yards short of it. If you go for it with your second and hit a poor shot, it's difficult to get a birdie out of it. The problem is that if you actually bail out too far left off the tee, it's quite easy to fail to carry the ditch and the bunker with your second shot. You could then be hitting as much as a six-iron in for your third, and the hole starts to become a bit of trial. It is a good par five, but just a little too dominated by the distance you hit it off the tee at times.

HOLE 18
The eighteenth is the hole where the Americans kept hitting it into the water in 1989, although I'm not too sure why. Perhaps it was pressure as much as anything else. It is probably getting easier as the years progress because everyone's hitting it further. In years gone by, any sort of tee shot right of where you were aiming meant you were going in with either your longest iron or wood. Now, with the power and the technology at the disposal of modern players, it's quite often just a three-wood and a five-iron to the middle tier. I don't think you'll see the pin on the front tier because there's just a bit too much slope there. Of course the hole is at its toughest with the pin on the very back tier. It narrows down towards the back and you have to hit a pretty accurate iron shot to get it on that section of the green.

23. BACK TO THE FUTURE

The Ryder Cup has always been my principal target and has always brought the best out of me, for one simple reason. It became fairly apparent early in my career that winning a major championship was unlikely to happen, even though I wasn't a million miles away a couple of times at the Open, so looking back on my career to date I can have few regrets. Given the level of talent I had, I believe I have made as much as I could out of it, because to win a major championship you need a certain type of game and in one crucial area I was found wanting. Apart from having to be a good player in the right place at the right time, you need a finely honed short game and you must be a very good putter. I have been a decent putter at times, sometimes for two or three holes at a time, but I've never been consistent enough often enough to get close enough to the big prizes.

I've certainly never approached the standard of putting enjoyed by some of my British contemporaries, who in their prime were nothing less than sensational with the short stick. Nick Faldo has always had what it takes with the putter in his hands, ditto Sandy Lyle, or in his case certainly through to the early 1990s. Probably the only European I have seen win a major who wasn't an outstanding putter was Ian Woosnam, who has been decent but certainly not as good as some of the others. I was reasonable most of my career, but you need something special on the greens if you're to win a major. Colin Montgomerie has for several years done everything but win a grand slam title, losing play-offs for the US Open and the US PGA, though in his case I think he's been unlucky, simple as that. Nonetheless, it just has not happened for him, and the same can be said of Phil Mickelson.

Looking to the future can be a dangerous thing, but it seems reasonably certain that I will try my luck in America, not because McDonald's have opened a string of fish and chip shops, but for no other reason than that the rewards on their Seniors Tour are astronomical. I have the choice at the end of 2003 either to play the European Seniors or to go to America and try to get my card. It's something I've still not decided, but if I opt for the USA then it would mean spending quite a lot of time over there and I would only be prepared to do that if I was playing well enough. I can always just stay and play in Europe where the money has got bigger over the last couple of years, certainly enough to make a decent living. To fill the gaps I could perhaps do a bit of television commentary as well, but quite a lot depends on my outside business interests. If they grow in the next couple of years, then I would be tempted just to stay in Europe.

I'm involved in course design with my partner Andrew Mair, and we recently hooked up with a company called Golf Plan run by a chap called Ronald Fream, who has designed many courses around the world. I've only done two courses to date: 18 holes at a place called Matfen Hall in Newcastle and 27 holes at High Legh, which is very close to Mere in Cheshire. On top of that we've undertaken a number of alterations and additions, and re-designs of bunkers. We've not been pushing it too much because we've both had other things to do – Andrew is currently running Burgham Park, near Morpeth, a golf club we part own.

But the greater possibility, I feel, is that I will take the plunge in America, on what is something of an unpredictable Tour because people who have done extremely well on it are not always those who have had prolific careers on regular tours – people like José Maria Canizares, Vicente Fernandez and John Bland, to name but three. Canizares never really won much after becoming a Ryder Cup player in 1989, but his ball striking was still consistently crisp throughout his forties. He carried this form on into a Seniors career in America where he has made an absolute fortune. The Argentine Fernandez did the same, Blandy as well. Age did not stop them striking the ball as well as they had in their prime. This is encouraging for somebody like me because I feel I can be in that sort of bracket. I know my nerve is still basically sound, and if my health holds out, well, who knows, I may just be able to earn enough to keep my garden in good shape and Jane and me out on the ski slopes. I would hope to do reasonably well on a Seniors Tour, whether it's in America or Europe. I'm sure I'd enjoy it either way, and I certainly wouldn't be viewing a missed three-foot putt as the end of the world. My illness in the autumn and winter of 2000/01 put golf totally into perspective.

The Ryder Cup, though, will definitely continue to be a part of my life, as it will for those of many of my contemporaries. Sam Torrance's successor will probably not be determined until after the 2002 match. I have said elsewhere that I believe Nick Faldo could make a good captain, but I think in most players' eyes Ian Woosnam and Bernhard Langer are seen as the next likely leaders. I don't think Woosy will wait until the Ryder Cup comes to Wales before accepting; at 53 he'd be on the Seniors Tour by then and would have lost touch with quite a lot of the Tour players. Neither, I believe, will Bernhard wait until a Ryder Cup is played in Germany; he could be into his mid-seventies by then.

They would be the popular choices, in what order I don't know, but there would be a strong case for picking Bernhard when the match returns to America in 2004. His wife is American and he lives there a lot of the time. It might be a smart move to use that to help allay any crowd trouble, because they say the crowds in Detroit are even more fickle than the ones in Boston. Americans have huge respect for Bernhard, not least because he has twice won the US Masters, although I'm sure he would swap one of those for an Open.

Having Bernhard lead Europe in Detroit would leave Woosy in line for the K Club in County Kildare in 2006. I think it's unlikely an Irish captain will be chosen for that match, although if anyone had a claim it would probably be the evergreen Des Smyth. He knows the players very well, which counts for a lot among them, and he still plays at a good number of tournaments, so with regard to what is happening on the Tour he has his finger on the pulse. The trouble, though, is that by the time the Ryder Cup is at the K Club, Des will be three years into the Senior Tour. Having a captain from the Seniors Tour may be something that will happen in the future, but with the money in that area growing all the time, particularly in America, I think it's unlikely a player over 50 would forgo a career on the Seniors Tour to be a Ryder Cup captain – the stakes are probably too high. The same applies to Eamonn Darcy, and I suspect captaincy may be something he wouldn't like, although I honestly haven't spoken to him about it.

He is a similar age to Des and would also be on the Seniors Tour come 2006. So, overall, I think the next two captains will very probably be Langer and Woosy, and not necessarily in that order. After that it may well be the turn of Nick Faldo, who at the time of the appointment would still just about be on the regular Tour, or Monty, who would be 43, though I suspect his unique action will still be superbly constructed and well-oiled even in 2008.

Who Europe's future leaders will be no one really knows, but we do know where the Ryder Cup is going in Europe up to 2014. The decision for the 2010 venue was postponed a couple of times, probably because the Ryder Cup Committee had to be entertained at prospective venues so that they could take a proper and balanced decision. When it finally came, it was one most of the Tour wanted and expected, one which saw Celtic Manor, just off the M4 at Newport, getting the vote. The players thought it was right it should go to Wales for the first time, not only because they had had several Ryder Cup players, but also because Ireland had got the nod for 2006.

Celtic Manor is, in my view, plenty good enough. It certainly knocks spots off the new course at Gleneagles, which has been named as the venue for the 2014 match. I believe Celtic Manor is a better design, in better condition, has better practice facilities and hotel, and is easier to get to. The owner, Terry Matthews, is also going to build some new holes so that the slightly weaker ones can be dispensed with, so in my view there's no contest as to which is the better venue. It makes me chuckle when people talk about Celtic Manor not being fit for the Ryder Cup. Just look at the Belfry. We played the Ryder Cup there in 1985, 1989 and 1993 and it wasn't a patch on what Celtic Manor is like at the moment – and that's over eight years before the Ryder Cup is due to be played there.

There has to be a lot of negotiations going on behind the scenes with regard to the Ryder Cup venue. Celtic Manor was, strictly speaking, the PGA's choice for the 2010 match and not the Tour's, because choice of venue has been alternating between the two parties. So taking it to Gleneagles in 2014 was probably some form of bargaining chip. The Tour played Gleneagles in 2001. It rained the Sunday before the tournament, but although we had pretty good weather after that it was still soaked the following Sunday. Not only is it vulnerable to water, it is also long and unsubtle in a number of places. The first eight holes I think are really good, but after that it's almost as if the course designer couldn't be bothered to pull out the stops for the last ten holes, deciding just to plonk them in where it was most convenient and leave it at that. Still, over twelve years to go . . .

It looks as if the match is going to be taken to the Continent again from 2018, but the problem with that is that there are very few suitable venues on mainland Europe, although there's plenty of time to create acceptable ones. They will have to, because at the moment big well-designed courses with the right amount of space and a very good hotel on course or very close by are few and far between. Head of the queue to be hosts in 2018 should really be Sweden, because I think they have had more Ryder Cup players than any other mainland country, with perhaps the exception of Spain, and we all trooped off to the land of Seve in 1997.

The trouble with Sweden is that winter starts a few weeks before summer ends – or, as my former coach Gavin

Christie used to say about Scotland, 'Six months of bad weather and then winter sets in.' The Scandinavian Masters is held in early August and generally has a bit of sunshine, but you can't hold a Ryder Cup then without getting uncomfortably close to the USPGA Championship. Certainly September shouldn't be a problem on the daylight front, because they're not that much further north than Scotland. I suppose they don't have anything approaching a suitable venue at the moment, so one would have to be built from scratch. I think the same could probably be said of Germany, although they have more in the way of good courses. Finding one in the right place with the right hotel, though, would be more difficult. France is a possibility, but they don't have a great Ryder Cup history, so I think we're looking at either Sweden or Germany.

The other thing about the Ryder Cup, personally speaking, is that it has allowed me to play against and see just about all the great golfers of the modern era. Unfortunately I never had the opportunity to play against Sam Snead, but I did see him in Switzerland one year – my first year as a professional, I think – and what a lesson it proved. Ken Brown and I were watching him give a clinic after his round and he went through all the clubs in his bag. When he pulled out his driver he hit a few off the tee. It was great to watch because he had a wonderful rhythm and a huge shoulder turn, and made it look effortless. He hit a few perfect drives, and then he hit one off the deck which was beautifully low and straight. 'I'm now going to hit a high driver off the deck,' he announced. Well, Ken and I couldn't have got three-woods in the air off the deck, let alone a driver, so we looked at each other, shook our heads and just couldn't see him doing it. We stood there with our mouths open as he hit this driver and the ball went dead straight up into the air. It was an unbelievable shot. It was the only time we ever saw Snead play, but it was nice to get a look at one of the legends of the game while he was still hitting the ball well. He would have been in his sixties then.

Generally, I think the Tour is in good hands. The biggest problem will come when executive director Ken Schofield retires. He has been at the job a long time now and it's fair to say, with the exception perhaps of the Gang of Four – Ballesteros, Faldo, Olázabal and Langer – he has the almost complete support of the players, the committee and the board, but there will come a time when he will step down and finding a successor to do the job as well as Ken did it may prove difficult. There's the option to bring in someone else from outside, but we always have George O'Grady, Ken's right-hand man. George is extremely capable, so that would certainly be a possibility. Bringing in people from different sports will be difficult. There's only one European Tour and finding someone with expertise in that field who hasn't been with the Tour a long time could be tricky. On the other hand, finding sponsorship these days is slightly different to running the Tour, so maybe the right person could be found, but it's difficult for anybody to know who is right for the job, i.e. someone who can go with their instincts a bit. Generally the Tour has long-term sponsors, which is something we are always looking to find. To be in a situation where you chop and change a lot is too volatile. If Ken does go and George is still around, he's the obvious choice in my book.

The Tour has made such huge strides in the last two decades, particularly with regard to player facilities. Not only are the courses bigger and tougher, they're also unrecognisable to those of twenty years ago in terms of condition. The greens are generally of a very high standard. If we get a week when they are less than good, it's a shock. The bunkers are always better, the practice range is now usually big enough to accommodate the Tour, we have chipping greens and practice bunkers most weeks, and all these things contribute to higher standards. It's one of the reasons why we compete pretty much on an even basis in Ryder Cups now. I think the change has been as much due to the players demanding better facilities as it has to Ken Schofield and everyone producing them. It can take quite a long time to turn things around, and without doubt twenty years ago facilities and golfers were not good enough, but now we have some really great venues and top-class courses in perfect condition, with the players to match.

Hopefully I'll be going forward with the Tour, but there's one place I don't want to visit again. Been there, seen it, done it, got the T-shirt and the scars to prove it. It didn't happen on a golf course, but I did lose a ball.

24. JANE'S STORY

During all the furore that followed the publication of *Into the Bear Pit*, I was busily trying to discover why so many people who had not even read the book were condemning Mark out of hand – and indeed, why he had been made to resign as Sam's assistant at the 2001 Ryder Cup when he was diagnosed with cancer. Surprisingly, the whole weak-kneed bunch of them ceased to have the remotest significance in our lives.

I had been a little concerned about Mark's health throughout 2000. He kept complaining of back ache, which for him is fairly unusual. Knees, elbows, wrists yes, but very rarely back pain. Things came to a head when he joined my sister Liz and I for a run one morning in late summer. Although an infrequent runner, Mark is one of those annoying people who are naturally fit and although Liz and I were running up to seven miles quite regularly at that time, whenever he joined us he would always sprint the last couple of miles to 'get my heart rate up'. On this occasion he had to stop and rest because of a pain in his back. I knew then that something was definitely not right.

After going back and forth to the doctor and there being no sign of improvement, it was decided that Mark should go for a scan. I was not best pleased when he said he couldn't have this done for a fortnight because of his tournament commitments. I was desperate for him to cancel everything and find out what was wrong. The scan was duly booked for Monday, 2 October 2000.

I remember sitting in the waiting room at Harrogate hospital and hearing the doctor who had done Mark's scan muttering to an assistant something with 'Mark James' in the sentence. He then asked her, 'Is that his wife?' and disappeared through a door behind the receptionist's screen. I felt sick then, and do now just thinking about it. Mark then emerged to tell me there was something that looked like lymphoma behind his stomach and what's more, it was the size of a rugby ball.

We held hands in the car all the way home and uttered not one word. It was a beautiful sunny autumn afternoon and a close friend's birthday. We dropped a card through the door on the way, and I remember thinking, 'Please don't let there be anybody in. I don't want to talk to anybody.' We didn't even talk about it when we got home. I think we knew how the other was feeling and talking about it wasn't going to make it go away.

Although we didn't really feel like speaking to anybody, practicalities had to be taken care of. Our families had to be told, of course, and Mark had several golf days and appearances lined up for the next couple of weeks, which obviously had to be cancelled or postponed. Since he couldn't really say, 'Sorry, but I'm going to be ill for a week on Thursday,' we were forced to tell everyone more than we would have wished at that time, since we really didn't know exactly what the problem was ourselves yet. As a result, the press were on to us like a ton of bricks. One reporter from the *Yorkshire Post* group asked to speak to Mark the very next morning. When I said he was unavailable and after confirming that I was indeed Mark's wife, he said, 'Well listen, I've heard he's battling stomach cancer. Is it true?' I know the press are renowned for not letting the truth get in the way of a good story, but this seemed insensitive in the extreme.

The next couple of weeks were a really bad time for both of us. I just felt sick. I have always been able to eat under any circumstances. If I feel ill, it might make me feel better, if I'm fed up, something to eat might cheer me up, if I'm happy, it's a celebration, any excuse to eat and drink in our family. However, at this point, I really could not get anything past my lips. Mark didn't seem to have the same problem in that respect, although he couldn't fit much food into his stomach because of the size of the tumour behind it.

It didn't feel like it at the time, but things moved fairly quickly after that first awful Monday. On Tuesday, 3 October he was whipped into Leeds for another, more comprehensive scan, followed that afternoon by biopsies and a bone marrow extraction. Because these tests proved inconclusive, he was back in hospital a week later for what turned out to be a much bigger operation than either of us had realised. I waved him off to theatre at the Leeds General Infirmary, expecting to see him a couple of hours later with a small hole in his tummy, sitting up in bed drinking a cup of tea! Having been told that he should be back in his room by 3.30 that afternoon, I went off to meet Liz and her daughter, my then three-year-old niece, Grace, for lunch in Harvey Nichols. Since there wasn't time for me to go home and back again, they came into Leeds to keep me company for a couple of hours. Needless to say, I was back in Mark's room at 3.30 p.m., where I spent two more hours waiting for him to come back from surgery, imagining the absolute worst. One of the nurses came in with a cup of tea for me, by which time I couldn't stop crying. She said, 'Look, let's just get him back here and over this operation and then you can face whatever has to be faced.' She was so lovely to me, but, honestly, I did not want to hear what she was saying. It wasn't a case of 'facing what had to be faced', it was simply a matter of getting him better. I knew nobody could tell me that, but it was all I wanted to hear – and all I would hear.

Paul Finan, Mark's surgeon, eventually tracked me down in Mark's still-empty room, to tell me that the op had gone well, that he hadn't found anything unexpected and the reason Mark was so late back was that he wasn't settling well following his anaesthetic. Boy, was that the truth. What followed was the longest night of our lives. He had a fourteen-inch scar down his front, was still suffering awful back pain from the tumour pressing on his spine and reacting incredibly badly to the morphine he'd been given for pain relief. It seemed that the nurses had to move him every five seconds to help get him comfortable. They kept telling me he wasn't in as much pain as it seemed, but I found that very hard to believe. He was moaning and groaning and thrashing about, and there was nothing I could do to help except to keep fetching the poor nursing staff in to move him yet again.

It was unbelievably hard to sit there every day, waiting for the results from the latest biopsy, aware that Mark was still in considerable discomfort, feeling lousy and obviously scared to death. I used to wait until he fell asleep, which was fairly regularly, then go and sit on the loo and bawl my eyes out until he woke up. I have never felt so utterly exhausted in all my life.

If sitting with Mark all day was hard, leaving him at night was even harder. Right from the beginning, whenever Mark was in hospital, I moved into Liz's spare room. She, her husband Mark, known to all as Waddy (to avoid years of confusion, our respective Marks are Jess and Waddy), and Grace were absolutely what got me through those awful five months. I used to feel very guilty leaving Mark on his own while I went home to close family and a strong gin and tonic. Although Gracie was always in bed by the time I got home, she didn't half cheer me up at breakfast, by which time I'd usually been awake for at least four hours.

Another broken promise! I always swore never to have a mobile phone, but relented when Mark went into hospital and have to admit that it proved extremely reassuring when I could speak to Liz on my way back to the car in the dark every evening. Reassuring for both of us, because I think Liz was convinced I was going to be mugged in the LGI car park. I would make all the necessary phone calls on the mobile and then cry all the way home. Home to the Waddys' that is, as I could cheerfully have put a match to our own house just a mile up the road. I called in every morning to shower and pick up the post, but it felt so empty. Very strange really when you consider how much time I spend there on my own normally.

Another strange feeling I had at the time was that of having done something 'wrong'. I almost felt too guilty to go even to Tesco's. I felt as if everyone was looking at me but dare not speak. If Mark had broken his leg or had the flu, everyone would have approached me to ask after him, but because cancer is still such a taboo subject, many people don't know what to say, so they say nothing and simply avoid you. I know now that the best thing to do is grasp the bull by the horns and ask the questions you are most afraid of asking. 'How is so-and-so and the how the hell are you coping with it all?'

It's very difficult to describe how I felt during those first few weeks. I definitely wasn't shocked by the diagnosis – I knew something was seriously wrong with Mark. I would be lying if I said that I had never contemplated the worst, but I honestly never, ever thought for one second that it would really come to that. Waiting for the final and proper diagnosis was the worst and longest time of all. At first it was thought to be lymphoma, 'very treatable' and hadn't Paul Azinger recovered from that perfectly well? Then it wasn't lymphoma but they didn't really know what it was and, worst of all, where it had come from. The relief when Paul Finan came to tell us that it was probably testicular in origin, and one of the most responsive cancers to chemotherapy, was indescribable. He also said that Mark's symptoms should disappear within a few days of commencing treatment, good news at last. That was the first time we actually cried together.

The next hurdle to overcome was our first trip to the Cookridge Cancer Centre. This was a place I had driven past hundreds of times in my life, never once without hoping I would never have to go there. Well, there we were and although Mark's oncologist, Bill Jones, and all the nurses and staff at Cookridge were extremely confident and reassuring, we were both still absolutely dreading the chemotherapy. We had very little idea what to expect, except the worst. In fact, apart from feeling tired, because the treatment was delivered throughout the night, Mark's only problem was that he still hadn't fully recovered from his operation a mere fortnight before. In fact, as promised by Paul Finan, the symptoms of the tumour disappeared within a few days of his first chemo session. However, although he was tolerating the chemo exceptionally well, it was quite difficult for me to appreciate just how ill Mark really was. Bill Jones was anxious for him to get some exercise, walking short distances, maybe to the end of the drive and back. It sounded ridiculous to me that a man who walks miles every day for a living should only be able to make it to the end of the drive, surely he couldn't be that ill! He was though; we'd set off to the end of the road, with Mark begging me to slow down. Under different circumstances I would have thoroughly enjoyed that request! Not being the most patient person in the world, I have to admit to finding this quite frustrating.

By Christmas 2000 we seemed to be through the worst of it. Mark was much fitter and his weight was going back up to normal. In fact, the staff at Cookridge were now surprised at his appearance, having only seen him as a ten-stone-something weakling, as he was before his first treatment. I also thought he was starting to look better, but apparently I was under a bit of a misapprehension. We went to Liz and Waddy's for pre-dinner drinks on Christmas Day and, although nobody said anything at the time, all our family and friends who hadn't seen him throughout his illness said how shocked they were. What bit of hair he had on his head was now completely gone, along with his eyebrows, eyelashes and most of his moustache. Worst of all, we're all used to seeing Mark fairly tanned, or at least 'weathered', but he was so pale as to be nearly transparent. Eventually, during his final chemo at the beginning of January 2001, even the moustache had to go – it was looking too pathetic for words, so he shaved it off. Following another evening at the Waddys' (do you think they were sick of the sight of us by now?), Gracie was found under their dining table 'looking for Uncle Mark's moustache – it's dropped off'!

Christmas came and went, but the roller-coaster ride continued. Four lots of chemo might do it, or maybe five. Perhaps five or six and no more surgery? Eventually we settled for four lots of chemo and, joy of joys, another big op. At least this time we knew what to expect. Not that that was a huge consolation considering the trauma of the last one.

We went off to meet with the surgeons who would be performing the various procedures, expecting to be told that they would simply chop out the dead tumour, remove the offending testicle and repair a large hernia (don't ask!). However, they were suddenly discussing 'kidney transplants' and 'further treatment following the operation', just when we thought it was nearly all over with. Apparently the previous day's scan had shown the tumour to be cemented around the tubes leading to one of Mark's kidneys, making it impossible to remove a great deal of the tumour without him losing a kidney. They said they may have to remove and transplant his own kidney, rather than leave him with just the one. Otherwise, depending on the state of the tumour when they uncovered it, he may or may not need further treatment: radiotherapy or further chemo. All this information really came like a hammer blow and we felt as though we were back to square one. I know that by many people's standards, what we went through was really not too bad, but at this point I was beginning to wonder how much more we could take. Waiting for the second op was as bad as waiting for the first, not least because we remembered the state Mark came back from the theatre in.

No prizes for guessing where I spent the day while Mark was undergoing his second operation. Liz and I were waiting by the phone, jumping down the throat of anyone daring to ring who wasn't from the LGI. Eventually, after an extremely long five hours, Adrian Joyce (the surgeon for this operation) phoned to say that the procedure had gone much better than he had anticipated, that they had managed to remove most of the tumour and he felt fairly optimistic that what was left behind was dead. Another call came a few minutes later from Paul Finan, confirming what Mr Joyce had said and, to be honest, he sounded even more positive that the remaining tumour was well and truly necrotic – dead! This meant that what would probably happen next was that Dr Jones at Cookridge would just keep an eye on Mark at regular intervals, to make sure nothing sprang back into life, at which point they would be able to pounce on it immediately. However, everyone seemed to think it unlikely that further treatment would be necessary. All that worry over nothing! I headed for the hospital around 9 p.m. that evening, expecting to find Mark writhing in agony as before. However, although he was pretty groggy, he was awake and not in any pain, thanks to the two epidurals he had been given during the op. In fact he recovered indecently quickly this time and was home in less than a week.

That was the end of it really. The three-monthly scans are getting slightly less worrying. Although Mark doesn't seem to bother, I do still get into a bit of a stew over them. Whilst awaiting the results of one just before Christmas 2001, we were at a dinner party where a guy we've known for years was asking me about Mark's illness. He thought that Mark had been suffering from bowel or stomach cancer. I was quite happily telling him the whole story – I really don't mind talking about it – when for some reason

I started to panic. One minute I was telling Richard that Mark was absolutely fine and that there was nothing to worry about, the next minute I was fighting back the tears because we hadn't had the latest scan results yet and who knew what could have turned up. I felt a complete idiot to be honest, but had to control myself. Needless to say, the results of the scan were fine.

Some people seem to think this should have been a life-changing experience for both of us, but, in all honesty, it really hasn't been. It has taught us who our real friends are, some of whom drove eight hours in a day to see Mark either in hospital, or at home, or both. We even had friends who came for the weekend and insisted on staying in a hotel so as not to cause any extra work. We took photos that weekend, just before Christmas 2000, which were a bit of a shock when we had them developed – I think we still didn't appreciate how ill Mark was looking by then. Another eye-opener was when friends of ours came to see us over that same Christmas holiday. Gill, Dave and their children, Stephanie, then seven and Harrison, five, spent a great afternoon with us and Gill remarked how fantastic to be their age and completely unaware of anything being amiss. The next time I saw Steph, however, she took me to one side and asked where Mark was. She said she had been hoping to see him because 'he didn't look proper last time' and was he OK now? By this time, we pretty much knew that Mark was going to be fine, but I still could have wept buckets. Unaware, my eye!

My family did what they all do best. Having been told that Mark needed 'building up', my mum and dad made so many home-made pasty and cake deliveries that he had to go on a crash diet straight after his final op, or he was heading for velour leisure-suit land. My brother James was entertainments manager and introduced Mark to Harry Potter, amongst other things. Liz, Waddy and Gracie were my lifeline. I think Liz suffered every bit as much as I did, but she was absolutely positive throughout. It must have been difficult sometimes for her to keep cheerful all day for Grace's sake. In fact, Grace did ask her one day, 'Are you sad, Mummy?' However, Liz's catchphrase was 'We'll get him through it', and we did. We put our faith in medical science and the wonderful surgeons, doctors and nurses who did so much to help us both through a horrendous experience, which now almost seems as though it happened in a different life.

There are things we have learned though. For instance, previously, on hearing of someone's illness, bereavement or other trauma, I would step back, thinking it's none of my business, let them have their 'space'. Now, however, I would at the very least drop them a line, if only to say we're thinking of them. At first, the hundreds of cards and letters we received were fairly unwelcome, they confirmed that Mark was really ill. Flowers felt like wreaths and I wanted to put them straight in the bin. However, we soon began to appreciate everyone's concern, and the letters from people who had recovered from cancers of every type were incredibly encouraging. People even phoned Liz and my family to see how they were coping, which would probably have never occurred to me to do before, but we really appreciated little things like that, because all Mark and I could do was what was best to help ourselves through. Selfish though it seemed, even at the time, we just couldn't cope with anybody else's emotions.

As I am sitting writing this chapter, Mark is waiting for the results of his latest scan and look, I'm not panicking at all – except every time the phone rings.